A Pilgrim's
FATIMA
AND THE SURROUNDING AREA

By Andrew Houseley

Pilgrim Book Services Limited

© Pilgrim Book Services Limited and Andrew Houseley
ISBN 978-0-9569768-9-5

Published by Pilgrim Book Services Ltd., Regd. at 21 Birchwood Drive, Rushmere St Andrew, Ipswich Suffolk IP5 1EB, United Kingdom

 www.pilgrimbooks.com

First Edition 2017
Typeset and Design by Ivan Yonov
Original Cover designs by Fielding Design. Original Text design by Bob Vickers.
Maps by Kevin Baverstock. Adapted from Map data © OpenStreetMap contributors
Printed in Bulgaria by E Print Ltd

The publishers and author are grateful for the assistance of the following.
Santuário de Nossa Senhora do Rosário de Fátima, in particular: the Revd. Rector, the Information Office, the Mutimedia Archive and the Communications Department.
Postulation for the Cause of Canonization of the Blessed Francisco and Jacinta.
The Carmelite Sisters of Coimbra.
The Portuguese National Tourist Office in London: António Padeira. The Centro Portugal Turismo Region: António Belo and Marli Monteiro. The Lisboa Turismo Region: Vitor Cariço.
In Santarém: Vera Duarte, The Tourist Office, and Santuário do Santíssimo Milagre.
Every effort has been made to contact holders of material which appears in this book. The publishers and author apologise for any errors and omissions.
The Mass: Excerpts from the English translation of The Roman Missal © 2010, International Commission on English in the Liturgy Corporation. All rights reserved.
Photographs © Santuário de Fátima and © Andrew Houseley unless otherwise stated.

Cover picture: The crowned Statue of Our Lady of the Rosary of Fátima

CONTENTS

The Centre of Pilgrimage

Part 1
PREFACE

WHY PILGRIMAGE? WHY FÁTIMA?

This book is aimed at the visitor to Portugal, this country with so much to offer the traveller.

There is history in this former kingdom that sent out explorers to discover much of the world and spawned an empire that produced lavish riches. It has a wonderful climate, sandy beaches and a windswept coast, superb food and beverages, art and architecture. By all means, you are in Portugal to have an enjoyable holiday, and broaden the mind. The Portuguese are known for their gentle old-fashioned manners, welcoming smiles, and hospitality. Here, however, travel takes on added purpose as we make our pilgrimage.

We come to Fátima for reasons that combine into a whole. Why in this part of central Portugal? We come because in the early part of the 20th century, three illiterate shepherd children experienced the presence of God through Jesus' mother Mary. The other side of this question, is that we simply do not know why this area, and these children were chosen. We know that they were brought up well by their parents and were receptive to Christian teaching. This country, Portugal however, had already committed to the Immaculate Heart of Mary – the kingdom was solemnly dedicated to Our Lady Queen of Portugal by King João IV in 1646. As we shall see, this matters.

The remarkable apparitions, that mere children were chosen, the events that were foretold, and the miracle that was performed for all to see, gave rise to a vibrant tradition of pilgrimage that has only grown over the decades. The substance of the pilgrimage is the message of Fátima: firstly, you must pray; you must make sacrifices not merely for your own sins but for the sins of those who do not believe or do not acknowledge their sins. You may well come here to rediscover how to do this, to strengthen your own faith and the daily practise of it. That can be easier said than done: the lives of many visitors on arrival may be troubled, and at Fátima they can only fulfil its message as individuals having sought solace.

War is outrage and arises from the sins of humanity. The message of Fátima, secondly, is global, that wars and individual acts of violence can be prevented, or once started can come to an end having peaceful outcomes, but only through a greater manifestation of faith. So it comes back to prayer and penance, we must be thoughtful and truthful, and take away from our pilgrimage to Fátima a greater love of humanity and desire to serve God.

Pilgrimage, as of faith itself, is a deeply personal experience. Everyone who visits Fátima will gain their own unique impression, taking away lasting memories, and apply what they learn to their lives. Fátima welcomes all, including those of other faiths, and the curious searching for meaning. For not to do so, it is suggested, would be contrary to its message of peace. The Fátima story and message cannot fail to move anyone who discovers it. It takes its place in the worldwide act of pilgrimage, for the sake of peace, for the sake of humanity.

Andrew Houseley
May 13th – 15th 2017

Part 2
THE FÁTIMA STORY

The following is taken as its primary source the Memoirs of Sister Lúcia (Property of Postulation for the Cause of Canonization of the Blessed Francisco and Jacinta) available to order online or in person from the Sanctuary Bookshop http://loja.fatima.pt

Lúcia dos Santos was born on March 22nd 1907, the youngest of seven children, in the small village of Aljustrel, part of the parish of Fátima in the district of Ourém. This was a rural part of central Portugal, where families who had land lived off it, where wealth was scarce and poverty commonplace. Mortality was high at all ages, compared with modern standards. Lúcia's parents, António and particularly her mother Maria Rosa, made sure that the children received a Christian upbringing, and Lúcia received her first Holy Communion at the unusually young age of six. Family circumstances meant that from early 1915, instead of attending school, Lúcia had to tend the family's flock of sheep. She was joined later by her two younger cousins, Francisco (b. June 11th 1908) and Jacinta (b. March 11th 1910) Marto, who had been given the same duties for their family's flock. By 1917, in this isolated daily existence, the three children, illiterate and sent to work at a young age, saw almost no-one else between morning and evening. The terrain consisted of a high valley interspersed with olive groves, oaks, holm oaks and pines, leading up some hills. The sheep would graze on parcels of land the families owned, while the little shepherds played games, prayed the Rosary, and the girls danced while Francisco played his flute, or they sang popular songs.

APPARITIONS OF THE ANGEL

Prior to Francisco and Jacinta joining her, sometime in 1915, Lúcia was accompanied by three other local children, sisters Teresa and Maria Rosa Matias, and Maria Justino, on the southern slope of a hill called Loca do Cabeço. This recollection is rather vague – certainly compared with what was to follow. They were about to start praying the Rosary, when **they saw what appeared to be a cloud in human form**, whiter than snow, but without discernible features such as hands or eyes. The children continued praying while gazing up at the image; when they finished their prayer the image disappeared. After some time, the girls returned their flocks to the same location, and **on**

different days saw the same image twice more. Lúcia told her family, who mocked her and her mother dismissed the story as childish nonsense.

Later, in what was **probably the spring of 1916,** Lúcia set out with Francisco and Jacinta to graze their sheep at some land at the eastern foot of the Cabeço. It began to drizzle, so they climbed up to shelter under a rock in the middle of an olive grove. Long after the weather had brightened into a fine calm day, a sudden strong wind began to shake the trees. They looked up and saw what Lúcia likens to the same image as before, coming towards them. But this time, it drew closer and the children were able to see it was a young man, 14 or 15 years old, pure white and transparent as crystal when the light shone through. As the figure drew up to them, he said:

"Do not be afraid, I am the Angel of Peace. Pray with me." He knelt down and bowed his head until it touched the ground. The children followed and repeated his words:

"My God, I believe, I adore, I hope and I love You! I ask pardon of You for those who do not believe, do not adore, do not hope and do not love You!" Having repeated these words three times, the Angel rose and said:

"Pray thus. The Hearts of Jesus and Mary are attentive to the voice of your supplications." Then he disappeared. Lúcia recounts that the three were so immersed in the intense supernatural atmosphere, that they were scarcely aware of their own existence; they remained in the same spot for some time, repeating the prayer. The spirituality only began to dissipate the next day, but the children continued to spend many hours praying as they had been instructed to do.

Spring turned to summer, and in the heat of the siesta, the animals were returned to their pens while the children would shelter under the trees by a well behind Lúcia's house. It was here (Arneiro) that **the Angel appeared for the second time,** imploring them:

"What are you doing? Pray! Pray very much! The Hearts of Jesus and Mary have designs of mercy on you. Offer prayers and sacrifices constantly to the Most High."

"How are we to make sacrifices?" asked Lúcia.

"Make of everything you can a sacrifice, and offer it to God as an act of reparation for the sins by which He is offended, and in supplication for the conversion of sinners. You will thus draw down peace upon your country. I am its Angel Guardian, the Angel of Portugal. Above all, accept and bear with submission, the suffering which the Lord will send you."

Lúcia describes these words as, 'like a light which made us understand who God is, how He loves us and desires to be loved, the value of sacrifice, how pleasing it is to Him, and how, on account of it, He grants the grace of conversion to sinners.'

The children began to offer all that was displeasing to them, while continuing the prayer. In late September or early October, **the Angel appeared for the third time**. The three had been grazing the sheep in an olive grove called the Pregueira, and decided to climb up to a hollow among the rocks to pray, going around the hill to get to it. They knelt down with their heads touching the ground, as they had been taught, repeating, 'My God, I believe, I adore, I hope and I love You ...' several times when an extraordinary light shone down on them. They jumped up to see the Angel holding in his left hand a chalice, with the Host suspended above it, from which drops of blood fell into it. Leaving the chalice suspended in the air, the Angel knelt down beside Lúcia, Francisco and Jacinta and made them repeat three times:

"Most Holy Trinity, Father, Son and Holy Spirit, I adore You profoundly, and I offer You the most precious Body, Blood, Soul and Divinity of Jesus Christ, present in all the tabernacles of the world, in reparation for the outrages, sacrileges and indifference with which He Himself is offended. And, through the infinite merits of His most Sacred Heart, and the Immaculate Heart of Mary, I beg of You the conversion of poor sinners."

The Angel then took the Host and the chalice, giving the Host to Lúcia and the contents of the chalice to Jacinta and Francisco, saying:

"Take and drink the Body and Blood of Jesus Christ, horribly outraged by ungrateful men! Make reparation for their crimes and console your God." Again he prostrated himself on the ground and repeated 'Most Holy Trinity ...' and then disappeared. Francisco and Jacinta had not yet received their first Holy Communion, and indeed never regarded this as a sacramental Communion. The three remained prostrate, repeating the new prayer again and again until darkness.

Lúcia and her cousins resolved not to tell anyone about the apparitions, while continuing to pray and make sacrifices. Lúcia's two eldest sisters married and therefore left home. Her father fell in with bad company and increased his drinking, resulting

Lúcia dos Santos & Francisco and Jacinta Marto (Wikimedia Commons)

in the loss of some of the family's property. Two more of Lúcia's sisters were initially sent away to work as servants. Lúcia's mother suffered from these sad times, to the extent it badly affected her health. There was some respite for mother from the medical treatment that she received. Meanwhile, Portugal's involvement in the Great War intensified, and Lúcia's brother was called up to the Front. Another pair of hands unavailable further threatened the family livelihood, but his godfather intervened with the doctor who examined the young man, and he was spared from military service.

APPARITIONS OF OUR LADY

On May 13ᵗʰ 1917 the three children were playing high up on the Cova da Iria, a hollow wide plateau that included dos Santos family land, where they regularly pastured their flock. At around Midday, they saw what they assumed to be a flash of lightning, and began moving the sheep down the slope towards shelter. About half way down, they drew almost level with a large holm oak tree, when they saw another flash. A few steps further on, they saw in front of them on a small holm oak a Lady dressed in white, shining more brilliantly than the sun, radiating an intense and clear light that shone on them. She spoke to the children:

"Do not be afraid. I will do you no harm."

"Where are you from?" asked Lúcia.

"I am from Heaven"

"What do you want from me?"

"I have come to ask you to come here for six months in succession, on the 13ᵗʰ day, at this same hour. Later on, I will tell you who I am and what I want. Afterwards, I will return here a seventh time."

"Shall I go to Heaven too?" asked Lúcia.

"Yes, you will."

"And Jacinta?"

"She will go also."

"And Francisco?"

"He will go there too, but he must say many rosaries."

Lúcia then asked about two girls who had come to her house to learn weaving, but had died recently. "Is Maria das Neves in Heaven?"

"Yes she is."

"And Amélia?"

"She will be in purgatory until the end of the world. Are you willing to offer yourselves to God and bear all the sufferings He wills to send you, as an act of reparation for the sins by which He is offended, and of supplication for the conversion of sinners?"

"Yes, we are willing."

"Then you are going to have much to suffer, but the grace of God will be your comfort." The Lady opened her hands and showed them a light so intense, that its rays penetrated their hearts and the innermost depth of their souls, showing themselves in God, Who was that light, more clearly than in the best of mirrors. Then they fell to their knees, repeating without speaking, "O most Holy Trinity, I adore You! My God, my God, I love You in the most Blessed Sacrament!"

The Lady spoke once more: "Pray the Rosary every day, in order to obtain peace for the world, and the end of the war." Then she began to rise towards the east, the light surrounding her seeming to open up a path in the firmament; the children later said that it seemed as though heaven opened.

The three seers vowed not to tell anyone what they had seen. But word got out concerning the apparition and the promised reappearances. Lúcia's mother and sisters treated the revelations with contempt, insisting that she was lying, causing more tension in the household and unhappiness for Lúcia. She could not meet her mother's demand that she admit to lying, for that would mean telling a lie, something that she had been brought up strictly not to do.

June 13th 1917 the Feast of St Anthony was a day of great festivities in the parish. Lúcia intended to go to the Cova da Iria after 10 o'clock Mass, having first put the flock out to pasture, thereby missing out on much of the day's celebrations. Several people from the surrounding area were waiting for Lúcia, so her brother came to call her back home while he took over watching the sheep. So she attended an earlier Mass and they accompanied Lúcia, Francisco and Jacinta to the Cova da Iria, asking a stream of questions along the way.

A number among the small crowd prayed the Rosary with the children. As soon as they had finished, the children saw a flash of light, and in a moment, the Lady was in front of them on the small holm oak.

"What do you want of me?" asked Lúcia.

"I wish you to come here on the 13th of next month, to pray the Rosary every day, and to learn to read. Later, I will tell you what I want." Lúcia asked for the cure of a sick person: "If he is converted, he will be cured during the year."

Then Lúcia requested: "I would like to ask you to take us to Heaven."

"Yes, I will take Jacinta and Francisco soon. But you are to stay here some time longer. Jesus wishes to make use of you to make me known and loved. He wants to establish in the world devotion to my Immaculate Heart. I promise salvation to those who embrace it, and those souls will be loved by God like flowers placed by me to adorn His throne."

"Am I to stay here alone?" asked Lúcia, sadly.

"No, my daughter. Are you suffering a great deal? Don't lose heart. I will never forsake you. My Immaculate Heart will be your refuge and the way that will lead you to God." Like the so-called 'Secrets' of Fátima to be revealed a month later, the children felt compelled not to tell their fates and of the world's devotion.

As she finished, just as before, the Lady opened her hands and showed the children rays of intense light, seeing themselves in that light as though immersed in God. This time, however, Jacinta and Francisco appeared to be in that part of the light which rose towards Heaven, while Lúcia was in that part which poured out on the earth. The Lady showed them in front of her right hand a heart encircled by thorns that pierced it. They understood it to be the Immaculate Heart of the Virgin, outraged by the sins of humanity, and seeking reparation.

Soon afterwards, the **parish priest** took a closer interest and resolved to **question Lúcia**, much to the relief of her mother. After a long interrogation, the priest concluded that in a revelation from Heaven, it was usual for Our Lord to tell the seer to give an account to the priest, whereas it seemed that Lúcia had resolved to keep it to herself. What she had witnessed, therefore, was a deception from the devil. But he kept an open mind as to what the future might reveal, and at all times was kind towards Lúcia. **Lúcia had doubts** she had seen the work of the devil and began to lose enthusiasm for making sacrifices, however, Jacinta and Francisco implored her that the devil was ugly, whereas the Lady was so beautiful and that they had seen her go up to Heaven. Lúcia had a dream in which the devil tried to draw her down to hell; she cried out to Our Lady for help, her screaming awakening her mother and sisters. She also resorted to hiding from her two cousins, weeping in solitary torment.

So, **July 13th 1917** drew near. By the evening before, Lúcia had even resolved not to go to the Cova da Iria. A large number of people had already gathered in preparation for the next day. Jacinta and Francisco had resolved to go without their cousin. Next day, Lúcia then felt compelled to go, and called at her uncle's house where she found the other two kneeling beside the bed crying. "Aren't you going then?" asked Lúcia.

"Not without you! We don't dare. Do come!"

"Yes, I'm going," replied Lúcia, whereupon her cousins' faces lit up with joy, and they set out together. They had difficulty working their way past the crowds of people who lined the roads, but arrived at the holm oak where many people were reciting the Rosary.

Once more, the children saw a flash of light and Our Lady appeared on the tree. Lúcia again asked Our Lady what she wanted of her, and again she was asked to come to the same spot on the 13th of next month, and to pray the Rosary every day in order to obtain peace for the world and the end of the war. Lúcia asked Her to work a miracle so that everyone would believe She was appearing.

She replied: "In October, I will tell you who I am and what I want, and I will perform a miracle for all to see and believe."

Some sick people had asked Lúcia to request the Virgin to cure them. She replied that it was necessary for these people to pray the Rosary in order to receive these graces. She concluded:

"Sacrifice yourselves for sinners, and say many times, especially whenever you make some sacrifice: O Jesus, it is for love of You, for the conversion of sinners, and in reparation for the sins committed against the Immaculate Heart of Mary."

As she raised her hands and radiated the light towards the earth, this time the children saw a sea of fire, with demons and souls in human form burnished from the flames, raised up by the flames and then falling back, shrieking and groaning in pain and despair. This terrified the children, who looked up to Our Lady, who said to them kindly but sadly: "You have seen hell where the souls of poor sinners go. To save them, God wishes to establish in the world devotion to my Immaculate Heart. If what I say to you is done, many souls will be saved and there will be peace. The war is going to end; but if people do not cease offending God, a worse one will break out during the pontificate of Pius XI. When you see a night illuminated by an unknown light, know that this is the great sign given you by God that he is about to punish the world for its crimes, by means of war, famine and persecutions of the Church and of the Holy Father. To prevent this I shall come to ask for the consecration of Russia to my Immaculate Heart, and the Communion of Reparation on the first Saturdays. If my requests are heeded, Russia will be converted, and there will be peace; if not, she will spread her errors throughout the world, causing wars and persecutions of the Church. The good will be martyred, the Holy Father will have much to suffer, various nations will be annihilated. In the end, my Immaculate Heart will triumph. The Holy Father will consecrate Russia to me, and she will be converted, and a period of peace will be granted to the world. In Portugal, the dogma of the Faith will always be preserved. Do not tell this to anybody except Francisco." Francisco, unlike Jacinta, saw but was unable to hear anything said by Our Lady (or the Angel before). These were the first two Secrets of which the children felt compelled not to reveal, but that they held secrets did quickly become known.

After each Mystery of the Rosary, Our Lady instructed them to say: 'O my Jesus, forgive us, save us from the fire of hell. Lead all souls to Heaven, especially those who are most in need.'

"Is there anything more that you want of me?" asked Lúcia.

"No, I do not want anything more of you today."

As before, Our Lady began to ascend to the east, until she finally disappeared in the immense distance of the firmament.

The parish priest questioned Lúcia again in front of her mother, trying to discover inconsistencies in her account, but at the end was at a loss as to what to make of it all.

On August 11th, two days before Our Lady was to appear again, Lúcia's parents and her aunt and uncle were summoned to bring the children to the Administrator of the District of Ourém, Artur Santos. It is a position that does not exist anymore, carrying with it a great deal of power and responsibility. While Lúcia's parents readily complied, her uncle refused to take Francisco and Jacinta with him, risking punishment. Santos tried to make Lúcia reveal the 'secret' and to promise never to return to the Cova da Iria, threatening various punishments, even death, if she refused. He got nowhere. When Lúcia returned home, she found Jacinta and Francisco praying for her; they thought she had been killed.

By **August 13th 1917,** again crowds in their thousands had poured in to the area, many with questions, others to plea for the children to intercede for the sick, and many leaving money. However, the Administrator had arrived at the Marto house and sent for Lúcia. When she arrived with her father, Santos was sitting in a room with her cousins. He interrogated them, trying again to extract the 'secret' and the promise not to return to the Cova da Iria. When, again, he got nowhere, he ordered Lúcia's father and uncle to take the children to the parish priest's house. It seems barely credible in our modern times, but, on the orders of the Administrator, the **children were taken** from the priest's house to what passed for the jail at Vila Nova de Ourém. They spent only a short time among the adult prisoners in the jail – whom they led in praying the Rosary – as this was another ploy by Santos to scare them; another was his telling the children that there was a vat of oil ready to boil them alive. The rest of their two days they spent in his home with his mother, where they were well looked after, before being returned to Aljustrel.

Santos, a manufacturer in the town, had founded a Masonic lodge and was keen to get on. The First Republic, established in 1910, was essentially anti-Clerical, with many of its supporters regarding the influence of religion as a block to progress and the advance of civic society. Meanwhile, this was also a time of immense problems created by the war effort, notably famine, all of which fell at the Administrator's feet. To add to this, there was the gathering public tumult at the events at the Cova da Iria – a febrile atmosphere. Of course, Santos' abduction of the seers was designed to disrupt the event of August 13th and accordingly, there was no apparition. The children returned home on August 15th. It proved to be a temporary interruption.

Four days later, **August 19th 1917,** Lúcia was accompanied by Francisco and his brother, João, with their sheep at a place called Valinhos. They sensed something supernatural, and thought Our Lady was about to appear. Lúcia gave João two coins so that he would fetch Jacinta. Meanwhile, Francisco and Lúcia saw a flash of lightning. Jacinta arrived and a moment later, they saw Our

Lady on a holm oak tree.

"What do you want of me?" asked Lúcia

"I want you to continue going to the Cova da Iria on the 13th, and to continue praying the Rosary every day. In the last month, I will perform a miracle so that all may believe."

"What do you want done with the money that the people leave in the Cova da Iria?"

"Have two litters made. One is to be carried by you and Jacinta and two other girls dressed in white; the other one is to be carried by Francisco and three other boys. The money from the litters is for the festa of Our Lady of the Rosary, and what is left over will help towards the construction of a chapel that is to be built here."

"I would like to ask you to cure some sick persons."

"Yes. I will cure some of them during the year." The expression on Our Lady's face turned to one of sadness, and she said: "Pray, pray very much, and make sacrifices for sinners; for many souls go to hell, because there are none to sacrifice themselves and to pray for them." She began to ascend as before, towards the east.

The Cova da Iria was vital to Lúcia's family livelihood. The crowds had destroyed some crops and grazing land for the sheep. Lúcia's mother, blaming her daughter, was forced to sell the flock.

September 13th 1917 arrived, and as Midday approached, Lúcia set out with Jacinta and Francisco for the Cova da Iria. The crowds were such (an estimated 30,000 is often given) that the children proceeded with difficulty, so many people shouting questions and some jostling others out of the way to get to the front. Many fell to their knees in front of the children, begging them to place petitions before Our Lady, most asking for cures, some to bring home sons from the war. They said yes to some, and helped up others, while a group of men went ahead to clear a path.

When they reached the holm oak, they began to say the Rosary with the people there, and shortly afterwards, there was a flash of light and Our Lady appeared on the tree.

"Continue to pray the Rosary in order to obtain the end of the war. In October Our Lord will come, as well as Our Lady of Sorrows and Our Lady of Mount Carmel. Saint Joseph will appear with the Child Jesus to bless the world. God is pleased with your sacrifices. He does not want you to sleep with the rope on, but only to wear it during the daytime." The children found the piece of rope in the road; it would have fallen off a cart. The children wore it round the waist as a mortification. Sleeping with it on would likely have caused the most discomfort.

Lúcia mentioned the requests for cures.

"Yes, I will cure some, but not others. In October I will perform a miracle so that all may believe." Then Our Lady began to rise, as before, and disappeared.

Estimates of the crowd range between 50,000 and 70,000 plus for **Saturday October 13th 1917** in torrential rain. This time, Lúcia's mother, torn with doubt and concerned for her daughter's safety, accompanied her along with her father. The opposition of those in authority was unabated, and there was a rumour that someone was going to explode a bomb at the moment of the apparition. They passed through the crowd, in scenes of supplicating piety, many kneeling, and many asking for intercession. Lúcia asked the people to close their umbrellas and say the Rosary. A short while later they saw the flash of light, and Our Lady appeared on the holm oak. A misty cloud, like incense, enveloped

"What do you want of me?"

"I want to tell you that a chapel is to be built here in my honour. I am the Lady of the Rosary. Continue always to pray the Rosary every day. The war is going to end, and the soldiers will soon return to their homes."

"I have many things to ask you: the cure of some sick persons, the conversion of sinners..."

"Some yes, but not others. They must amend their lives and ask forgiveness for their sins." Looking very sad, she added: "Do not offend the Lord

Thousands observed the Miracle of the Sun (Wikimedia Commons)

our God anymore, because He is already so much offended." Lúcia later remarked in her memoir: 'How loving a complaint, how tender a request! Who will grant me to make it echo through the whole world, so that all the children of our Mother in Heaven may hear the sound of her voice!'

The sky was still black with rain clouds. Our Lady opened her hands, and made them reflect on the sun, and as she ascended, the reflection of her own light continued to be projected on the sun. Lúcia was compelled to ask the people to look at the sun.

Then began what is often referred to as the **Miracle of the Sun**. Lúcia recounts:

'After Our Lady had disappeared into the immense distance of the firmament, we beheld St. Joseph with the Child Jesus and Our Lady robed in white with a blue mantle, beside the sun. St. Joseph and the Child Jesus appeared to bless the world, for they traced the Sign of the Cross with their hands. When, a little later, this apparition disappeared, I saw Our Lord and Our Lady; it seemed to me that it was Our Lady of Sorrows. Our Lord appeared to bless the world in the same manner as St. Joseph had done. This apparition also vanished, and I saw Our Lady once more, this time resembling Our Lady of Mount Carmel.' The children believed that they had witnessed expressions of the Joyful, Sorrowful, and Glorious Mysteries of the Rosary. Some members of the crowd say they saw snow, and rose petals.

The crowd as a whole saw the rain clouds part, to reveal the sun as a luminous disc. The sun began to flicker and move, shooting rays in different directions and illuminating objects and people in different colours as it did so. Then the sun stopped, and began to weave a dance, then fell towards the earth, making the people believe they were about to be wiped out; some called out to be saved, reciting acts of contrition. And yet some others said that they saw much less than this.

AFTER OCTOBER 1917

The parish priest complained that people were visiting the Cova da Iria and leaving money, while the church was under repair and short of funds. He eventually left the parish, unable to make progress. People, indeed, made regular visits, many wanting to question the children. Lanterns were kept burning day and night; some poles were erected to form an arch and crosses placed in the ground. The **Government remained opposed** and one night the poles were taken down, the holm oak dug up and towed away by car. However, they got the wrong tree. A chapel was built in 1919 at the place of the May, June, July, September and October apparitions by the holm oak, as Our Lady had instructed. On May 13th 1920, cavalrymen arrived in Fátima and tried to stop people going to the Cova da Iria. After intercepting Lúcia who was on her way there with a group, they took her home while attempting to frighten her. Eventually they all rode off, and by sunset that day, Lúcia and hundreds more were praying at the Cova da Iria. Mass was celebrated at the chapel for the first time on October 13th 1921. On March 6 1922, however, it was dynamited by the Ourém freemasons and partially destroyed, but reopened on January 13 1923. It remains the focal point of the Sanctuary today.

Lúcia's father António – previously always at the peak of health - had died on 31st July 1919 during a bout of double pneumonia. **Her mother fell seriously ill** and seemed close to death. Lúcia's sisters, still not convinced of what she had seen, but that she was the cause of all their misfortune, told her to go to the Cova da Iria and ask Our Lady to cure their mother. She did as they requested, and by the time she returned home, mother was already feeling better; three days later she got up and resumed the household duties. Lúcia had promised Our Lady that should her mother be cured, to go back with her sisters for nine consecutive days, on their knees from the road to the holm oak, and on the ninth day take nine poor children with them, and afterwards provide them with a meal. They fulfilled the promise, taking their mother with them. She declared: "How strange! Our Lady cured me, and somehow I still don't believe! I don't know how this can be!"

Having begun school, in late October 1918, **Francisco and Jacinta** saw their health deteriorate almost simultaneously. The 'Spanish Flu' pandemic that swept across Europe and reached other parts of the world from the start of 1919 lasted two years, claiming more lives than the casualties (dead and injured) of the Great War. On one visit, Lúcia asked Francisco:

"Are you suffering a lot, Francisco?"

"Yes, but I suffer it all for the love of Our Lord and Our Lady." Francisco died at home on April 4th 1919 aged 10.

Jacinta received visions of Our Lady, including the day and hour of her death. She had told Lúcia on another visit: "When I'm alone, I get out of bed to recite the angel's prayer. But now I'm not able to touch the ground any more with my head, because I fall over; so I only pray on my knees." Jacinta was later taken to hospital, first in Ourém and then in Lisbon, where she died on February 20th 1920 aged 9.One of the several priests who questioned the seers was **Canon Formigão** from Santarém. In July 1920 Lúcia spent a month in Lisbon initially with her mother, where at Dr. Formigão's instigation, a charitable lady, Dona Assunção, offered to pay for her education at a boarding school and put her up in the meantime. They accepted, but not long afterwards Lúcia went to Dr. Formigão's house in order to escape the inquiries of the Government, who had heard she was in Lisbon. She had been due to go to the Dorothean Sisters' school in Spain but, after returning to Aljustrel,

Bishop of Leiria, D. José Alves Correia da Silva

finally departed for the school of the same order in Vilar near Porto on June 16th 1921. Another reason, perhaps, for the delay was the arrival of the **Bishop of Leiria, D. José Alves Correia da Silva**, on August 5th 1920. The diocese had been re-established following a period in limbo that included the apparitions. He too questioned Lúcia, and recommended she go to Vilar because she was not known there. Initially cold towards the events, the Bishop bought the land at the Cova da Iria after consulting with local priests, and published the first book on Fátima written by Formigão. By that time, the Statue of Our Lady of the Rosary had been commissioned by Gilberto Fernandes dos Santos, from Torres Novas, sculpted by José Ferreira Thedim in Porto, blessed on May 13th 1920 in the Parish Church of Fátima, and brought to the Chapel one month later. Mass would be said at the Cova on 13th of every month from October onwards, however, pilgrimages continued to be prohibited by the Government. It was in October 1930 that the Bishop declared the visions of the three seers 'worthy of belief' and the following year all the Bishops of Portugal came to Fátima to consecrate the country to the Immaculate Heart of Mary.

It was on the eve of her departure to Vilar, that Lúcia says that she received the promised **Seventh Apparition**. Full of doubt about leaving, she went to the Cova da Iria; she felt Our Lady's hand touch her shoulder, looked up and beheld once again Her sweet voice:

"Here I am for the seventh time, go, follow the path along which the Bishop wants to take you, this is the will of God."

FURTHER APPARITIONS 1925-29

Lúcia herself stayed at the school from 1921 until October 1925, when she commenced the first formality of becoming a nun, being **admitted as a postulant** at the Dorothean Congregation in Pontevedra, Spain. Not long after entering the convent, on **December 10th 1925, Our Lady appeared to Lúcia in her cell** with a Child borne on a cloud. She revealed once more her Immaculate Heart surrounded by thorns.

The Child spoke: "Have compassion on the Heart of your Most Holy Mother, covered with thorns with which ungrateful men pierce it at every moment, and there is no one to make an act of reparation to remove them."

Our Lady said: "Look, my daughter, at my Heart, surrounded with thorns with which ungrateful men pierce me at every moment by their blasphemies and ingratitude. You at least try to console me and say that I promise to assist at the hour of death, with the graces necessary for salvation, all those who, on the first Saturday of five consecutive months, shall confess, receive Holy Communion, recite five decades of the Rosary, and keep me company for 15 minutes while meditating on the 15 mysteries of the rosary, with the intention of making reparation to me." This became known in shorthand as the **First Five Saturdays** appeal. However, when Lúcia told this to the Mother Superior, she said that, though she was prepared to propagate it, she alone could do nothing. On **February 15th 1926,** the Infant Jesus appeared to Lúcia again, in the yard of the convent, initially in the form of a child who she had seen in the same place and taught to say the Hail Mary. The child had had difficulty remembering, so Lúcia asked him to say: 'O my heavenly Mother, give me your Child Jesus!' The child transformed into the Infant Jesus and asked: "Have you spread through the world what our heavenly Mother requested of you?" Lúcia explained the difficulties.

Jesus replied: "It is true that your Superior can do nothing, but with my grace, she can do all." Lúcia repeated her confessor's opinion that this devotion already exists on the first Saturday of the month.

Jesus replied: "It would please me more if they did Five with fervour and with the intention of making reparation to the Heart of your heavenly Mother, than if they did Fifteen in a tepid and indifferent manner..."

Lúcia asked whether, because some people had difficulty confessing on a Saturday, it would be valid to go to confession within eight days.

Jesus replied: "Yes, and it could be longer still, provided that, when they receive Me, they are in the state of grace on the first Saturday, and had the intention of making reparation to the Immaculate Heart of Mary."

Lúcia then asked: "My Jesus! What about those who forget to form this intention?"

Jesus replied: "They can do so at their next confession, taking advantage of the first opportunity to go to confession."

Lúcia then moved to the convent at Tui in Spain in July 1926, and in October of that year **commenced her novitiate**. It was there that on December 17th 1927, she asked Jesus whether to write an account as she had been asked, and if the devotion to the Immaculate Heart of Mary should be included. Although there was no apparition, she received this reply:

"My daughter, write what they ask of you. Write also all that the Most Holy Virgin revealed to you in the Apparition [of June 1917] in which she spoke of this devotion."

In effect, Lúcia was given permission to reveal the intentions for Francisco and Jacinta to go to heaven and for Lúcia to stay for many years, and to make public the devotion to the Immaculate Heart.

It was on **June 13th 1929** that Lúcia, having taken first vows the previous year, was saying the prayers of the Angel in the chapel at Tui, which was lit only by a lamp. Suddenly, the whole chapel was illuminated by a supernatural light, and on the altar there appeared a cross of light which reached the ceiling. On the upper part of the cross, appeared the face of a man and his body to the waist, and on his chest, a dove. Nailed to the cross was the body of another man. His face and chest bore open wounds, with blood running down His body to drops of blood which fell down onto a large Host and into a chalice, suspended together in the air below the waist. Beneath the right arm of the cross was Our Lady of Fátima with her Immaculate Heart in her left hand, and wearing a crown of thorns and flames. Beneath the left arm of the cross large letters as of crystal clear water flowed down onto the altar, forming the words, "Grace and Mercy." Lúcia wrote: 'I understood that it was the Mystery of the Most Holy Trinity which was shown to me, and I received lights about this mystery which I am not permitted to reveal.'

Our Lady spoke to Lúcia: "The moment has come in which God asks the Holy Father, in union with all the Bishops of the world, to make the consecration of Russia to my Immaculate Heart, promising to save it by this means. There are so many souls whom the Justice of God condemns for sins committed against me, that I have come to ask reparation: sacrifice yourself for this intention and pray."

Lúcia wrote down the instructions of Our Lady - **in fulfilment of Her promise made in the apparition of July 13th 1917** - and passed it on. However, she later said she received an intimate communication from Our Lord, saying: "They did not wish to heed my request!... Like the King of France, they will repent and do it, but it will be late. Russia will have already spread her errors throughout the world, provoking wars, and persecutions of the Church: the Holy Father will have much to suffer." The reference to France appears to be an appeal to Louis XIV by Saint Margaret Mary in 1689 - a century before the

French revolution - after she received an apparition calling for the consecration of France to the Sacred Heart of Jesus. However, the king did not receive the appeal. It was only while under arrest in 1791 or 1792 that Louis XVI made the vow, but he had already lost the power to enact it and was guillotined in January 1793.

HEEDING OF THE APPARITIONS AND WARNINGS

Pope Pius XII

The first and second 'Secrets' or parts of the 'Secret' were revealed to the seers in the July 1917 apparition but not made known until Lúcia's Memoirs were published in 1942. As we have seen, the vision of hell (First Secret), consecration of Russia to the Immaculate Heart of Mary, the end of World War and the warnings of World War (Second Secret) and the abandonment of the Christian faith in favour of Communism by Russia were all foretold. On October 31st 1943, Pope Pius XII consecrated the world to the Immaculate Heart of Mary, making reference to Russia. The criticism which followed was twofold: that the Pope did not make the consecration with all of the bishops present, and indeed he made it in a radio address in Portuguese; secondly that the reference to Russia was not strong enough. Of course, by this time the world was engulfed by war, with the Soviet Union having entered on the side of the Allies. The Vatican – officially neutral, containing Fascist sympathisers, but in reality aiding the Allies - had previously concluded the Lateran treaty with Italy with Mussolini as Prime Minister. This was largely honoured, whereas a concordat with Nazi Germany was broken by systematic persecution of the Church. Outside the Vatican at the time of the broadcast, Rome was under Nazi occupation and had been bombed by the Allies. So, one could conclude that the Pope's address was an uncomfortable mixture of the highly symbolic and the politically expedient. The consecration of Russia was, nevertheless, incomplete and still further delayed. The times predicted in the apparitions were already well on the way to fruition!

THE 'THIRD SECRET' AND SAINT JOHN PAUL II

Saint John Paul II

The secrecy surrounding some of Our Lady's revelations to the seers, and their entrustment to the Church has, perhaps inevitably, led to considerable suspicion, resentment and misunderstanding in various quarters. Accusations abound of cover-ups and mishandling. However, as we have already seen, the children, and Lúcia in the confines of her life as a nun, were not permitted to reveal everything they had witnessed, with certain aspects being held back until further instruction had been received.

One further such aspect again concerns the apparition of Our Lady on July 13th 1917. After Lúcia became ill in 1943, with the other two 'Secrets' of this apparition having been published in her Memoir, the Bishop of Leiria asked her to write down this part of the apparition. It was written on January 3rd 1944 and kept in a sealed envelope at the bishop's palace with the instruction that it was not to be opened before 1960. In 1957, the Vatican ordered that all of Lúcia's writings be transferred there. Pope John XXIII requested the envelope in 1959; having read the contents possibly with his confessor they were re-sealed, without any comment. The same happened – or didn't to be precise – when Pope Paul VI read the contents with the Substitute, Archbishop Dell'Acqua, in March 1965. The Pope presided over the 50th anniversary of the apparitions in 1967, and asked Sister Lúcia to join him in Fátima. But the date of 1960 had passed: why the reluctance to publish, many have asked?

On May 13th 1981, the anniversary of the first apparition of Our Lady at Fátima, there was an **attempt on the life of Pope John Paul II** in St Peter's Square as he was making his way past crowds in the Popemobile. The assassin, Mehmet Ali Ağca, was restrained by several people, but all four bullets he discharged had hit the Pope. While recovering from his wounds, the Pope requested Sister Lúcia's text, and on July 18th was also handed a translation in Italian. Having read it, St John Paul II attributed his survival on that day to the protection of Our Lady of Fátima. He immediately made plans to visit Fátima as a pilgrim and give thanks, which he did on May 13th 1982. He also pledged to consecrate the world to the Immaculate Heart of Mary. This had been broadcast on May 7th 1981, but was repeated on his pilgrimage to Fátima. Later, on March 25th 1984, the Pope, having convoked all the bishops of the world, and with the Statue of Our Lady having been transported from Fátima to Rome, consecrated the world to the Immaculate Heart of Mary. Sister Lúcia confirmed that **it was this act of consecration that corresponded with what Our Lady has asked** in the apparition at Tui on June 13th 1929.

So, what was the third part of the 'Secret' or the 'Third Secret' that so moved the Pope? Lúcia recalls the vision thus:

'At the left of Our Lady and a little above, we saw an Angel with a flaming sword in his left hand; flashing, it gave out flames that looked as though they would set the world on fire; but they died out in contact with the splendour that Our Lady radiated towards him from her right hand: pointing to the earth with his right hand, the Angel cried out in a loud voice: 'Penance, Penance, Penance!' And we saw in an immense light that is God: 'something similar to how people appear in a mirror when they pass in front of it' a Bishop dressed in White 'we had the impression it was the Holy Father'. Other Bishops, Priests, men and women Religious going up a steep mountain, at the top of which there was a big Cross of rough-hewn trunks as of a cork-tree with the bark; before reaching there the Holy Father passed through a big city half in ruins and half trembling with halting step, afflicted with pain and sorrow, he prayed for the souls of the corpses he met on his way; having reached the top of the mountain, on his knees at the foot of the big Cross he was killed by a group of soldiers who fired bullets and arrows at him, and in the same way there died one after another the Bishops, Priests, men and women Religious, and various lay people of different ranks and positions. Beneath the two arms of the Cross there were two Angels each with a crystal aspersorium in his hand, in which they gathered up the blood of the Martyrs and with it sprinkled the souls that were making their way to God.'

The children said that they did not know which Holy Father the vision referred to, but were sad for him, and they suffered too. Sister Lúcia always repeated that it was a prophetic vision, but it was for others to interpret. She did, however, reaffirm her belief that the vision of Fátima concerned above all the **struggle of atheistic Communism against the Church and against Christians**, and described the sufferings of victims of the faith in the 20th century. For his part, the assassin, whom the Pope forgave, produced a stream of wildly conflicting accounts including that he was put up to the act by agents from the Eastern Bloc along with Turkish mafia, or by figures in the Vatican itself, or by Iran. As if to fuel the conspiracy theorists, the head of the KGB at the time of the assassination attempt, Yuri Andropov (later leader of the Soviet Union) wrote a letter to schoolteachers describing the Pope as 'our enemy' and calling for redoubling of efforts to atheise the youth. Saint John Paul II went on to be a key figure – according to some historians - in the collapse of the Communist system in Russia and Eastern Europe. In his native Poland, the Church undoubtedly played a role along with the Solidarity trade union, which he publicly supported. One of the bullets extracted from the Pope's body is attached to the inside of the crown worn by the Statue of Our Lady on anniversaries; a fragment of the Berlin Wall is displayed on the east side of the Sanctuary. **The third part of the 'Secret' was finally read out** by Pope John Paul II at Fátima in 2000.

But some theorists continued to propound that the Secret harboured a warning about a future catastrophe. If so, what does it predict, and when? On June 26th 2000 Cardinal Joseph Ratzinger, later Pope Benedict XVI, produced a theological commentary on the Message of Fátima. Again, frustration has been expressed, such as a perceived attempt to explain away the slowness of the Church to heed the messages and prophesies given in the apparitions. The document attempted to align the revelations of Marian apparitions to scripture. This is perhaps understandable. There are many centuries old chapels and grander shrines built where miracles occurred, for sure, but with Lourdes and then with Fátima and other sites before and since, we have the modern phenomenon, mass organised pilgrimage, with worship usually taking place away from – but not necessarily in place of - established churches at the locations where the revelations occurred. In the modern age,

Berlin Wall fragment

it is deemed important to the Church that modern pilgrimage does not sit outside it. Defining the visions as private revelations, the Cardinal explained what the children saw, and how they saw. The commentary was insistent that in the 'Third Secret' no definite future event was being predicted, rather it was a warning about what might happen if prayer and penance were not adhered to – like the vision of hell (First Secret). The text recalls First Peter (1:9): 'As the outcome of your faith you obtain the salvation of your souls.' And this is achieved by embracing the Immaculate Heart of Mary – a heart as the place where will, temperament and sensitivity all converge and it sees God fully – as the centre of your life.

THE CAUSES OF LÚCIA, FRANCISCO AND JACINTA

As Our Lady had foretold, Lúcia lived a long life as a nun. After Tui, in 1948 she entered the convent of Discalced Carmelites in Coimbra. She died on February 13th 2005 at the age of 97.

On February 13th 2008 Pope Benedict XVI waived the five-year waiting period established by ecclesiastical law before opening a cause for beatification. The Carmelo is the promoter of the cause of canonization of

Sister Lúcia answering correspondence in 2001 (©Carmelo de Coimbra)

Sister Lúcia. On February 13th 2017 the Bishop of Coimbra concluded his enquiry and initiated the next stage in the process, of sending instruction to the Congregation for the Causes of Saints in the Vatican. The postulator of the process, Fr Carmelita Romano Gambalunga said: "Blessed are the pure in heart, Lúcia was just that, a pure-hearted woman with a great mission in the twentieth century."
http://www.lucia.pt/?lang=en

The beatification of Francisco and Jacinta took place on May 13th 2000 with the Pope reading out the Third Secret. In March 2017 Pope Francis approved a miracle attributed to Blesseds Francisco and Jacinta Marto, who were asked in 2013 to intercede in the case of a Brazilian boy who suffered life threatening head injuries and proceeded to make a complete recovery. On his visit to Fátima the Pope canonized them at the Great Mass on the centenary of the first apparition of Our Lady May 13th 2017. They are the youngest saints not to have died as martyrs.

Part 3
SETTING THE SCENE

THE LAND AND THE PEOPLE OF PORTUGAL

Portugal lies in southwest Europe on the **Iberian peninsular,** bordered by about 900Km of Atlantic coastline to the west and south, and 1,200Km of land frontier with Spain to the east and north. From west to east in a straight line is never as long as 300Km. Portugal makes up one sixth of the peninsular, with Spain occupying nearly all the rest. Its three **major rivers** are shared with Spain: the Guadiana in the south; the Tagus which flows southwest, coming out at Lisbon; and the Douro across the north to Porto; also the Minho describes the short northern border. The north is mostly **mountainous** with relatively **high rainfall**, while the south is mainly **flat and dry**. Portugal also has two **island groups** in the Atlantic: Madeira and Porto Santo to the southwest, not far from northwest Africa; and further west the Azores. As a whole, the country enjoys up to 12 hours per day of **sunshine** in summer, with the southern Algarve justly popular as a destination for holidaymakers and retirees.

The Iberian peninsular has been inhabited from the **Neolithic and Palaeolithic** periods. The people who followed into Portugal include the Celtic **Lusitani** (although some scholars consider them Indo European) inhabiting a large area in the 1st millennium BC, along with the Gallaeci settling in the north, and several other Celtic and Iberian tribes. The **Ancient Greeks** discovered the Iberian peninsular about 500BC, and according to Portuguese legend, Odysseus founded a settlement above the mouth of the Tagus where Lisbon sits today. The Lusitani were the main foes of the **Romans**, as they established trading routes and ports such as Portus Cale – modern Porto – from which the country derives its name. After the Romans left in the 3rd century AD, Germanic tribes invaded. The **Suebi** were in turn conquered by the **Visigoths** in the 6th century, the development of whose early medieval Christian kingdom was interrupted in 711 by the Muslim **Moorish** occupations from North Africa. Their religion may have had fitful influence within *al-Ândalus*, but their advanced methods of crop cultivation, their language and Moorish art have influenced the whole peninsular down the centuries. The *reconquista* began in the north where the Visigoths had regrouped, with Alfonso III of Asturias

FÁTIMA is located in central western Portugal, in a transitory area between the mountains of the north and the plains of the south and east. There are large limestone deposits, many hills and mountains rising to 679 metres, barren landscape plateaus, and some famous caves. With moderate rainfall and warm summer sunshine, spring and early summer can be wet. It is only 40Km from the coast, and 130Km by road north from Lisbon (over an hour's journey).

Its early recorded history is shaped by Moorish occupation of the area around the principal town, Ourém. Legend has it that a Knight Templar named Gonçales Hermigues captured a Moorish princess named Fatima. She fell in love with her captor and converted to Christianity, taking the name Oureana, and they married. The town of Abdegas was finally recaptured in 1136 by King Afonso Henriques, whose daughter Teresa renamed it Ourém. The parish and main village of Fátima was also named in honour of the legend.

Due to the pilgrimage, a modern town has grown up surrounding and spreading out from the Sanctuary, leaving the original parish centre as a peaceful neighbour. There are a vast number of hotel beds, with a variety of activities having grown up to service the pilgrimage. The parish of Fátima today consists of several villages with a combined population of 11,800. Fátima itself is about 7,800 – but this as a whole includes a few villages such as Aljustrel.

sending his lieutenant **Vimara Peres** to expel the Moors and repopulate the area between the Douro and Minho, becoming the county of Portugal and Peres its first Count in 868. The capture of Cordoba in 1085 by Alfonso VI of León and Castile eventually allowed the kingdom of Portugal to be established and **Afonso Henriques**, on defeating the Moors in the south, to become its king in 1139. The Moors hung on in the Algarve and Alentejo but had finally left by the end of the reign of **Afonso III** in 1279.

DISCOVERIES, COLONIES, FASCISM AND DEMOCRACY

In 1373, Portugal and England made the longest lasting alliance in history, in which colonial target territories were divided up, and trading links begun, many of which survive today. However, when **Fernando I** died in 1383, his widow **Leonor** married off their daughter to Juan I of Castile, and promised the throne of Portugal to the offspring of the marriage. Fernando's illegitimate step-brother João led a revolt in which he was victorious and was crowned **João I.** The decisive battle took place very close to Fátima, at Aljubarrota and his superb monastery in honour of the victory can be visited. English archers were said to be have been decisive in the triumph of the much smaller forces loyal to João. He married Philippa of Lancaster, daughter of John of Gaunt of England, and the alliance was duly ratified at the Treaty of Windsor. It was their son **Prince Henry the Navigator** who began the great age of discoveries. He founded a school of navigation at Sagres on the southwest tip of the country, and prepared the voyages. The 15th and early 16th century discoveries included Brazil, an eastern route to India with perhaps Portugal's most famous son, **Vasco da Gama**, landing there in 1498, colonisation of parts of Africa, and the first trading links with China and Japan. Canada and even Australia are other claimed firsts. The **armillary sphere** – an early navigational aid – became one of Portugal's national symbols; you can spot it on the contemporary national flag. Two important treaties kept mostly at bay colonial rivalry with Spain. The trade in gold, precious stones and spices brought enormous wealth to Portugal, some of which is on display in the many palaces and more elaborate church architecture that can be seen today. If this all sounds too good to be true, then Portugal made up for it with much suspicion, prejudice and political instability. Jews expelled from Spain initially found a new home in Portugal among an already influential community, but as suspicion grew, they were

Departure of Vasco da Gama to India in 1497, by Roque Gameiro (National Library of Portugal) Creative Commons

Tomb of Henry the Navigator, Batalha

forced to undergo conversions as 'New Christians'. However this was not enough and they became one of the main targets of the Inquisition, an organisation installed in the 16th century by King João III and not finally disbanded until 1821. Accused heretics were publicly executed in *Autos-da-fé*.

By 1580, it was clear there was no Portuguese heir to the throne so Philip II of Spain, a grandson of Manuel I, became **Filipe I** of Portugal. During 60 years, the loss of independence led to involvement in war with the Dutch, strains in relations with England, and loss of some overseas territory. Decline was arrested by another national hero, the **Duke of Bragança**, who deposed the Spanish governor and became King João IV.

The Wars of Restoration with Spain were ended in 1668 by the Treaty of Lisbon. The reign of **João V** saw an 18th century gold rush in Brazil fund elaborate artworks and the building of his huge palace at Mafra. Five years after his death, in 1755, a massive earthquake devastated Lisbon and caused more destruction throughout the country. The inspirational Prime Minister, the **Marquês de Pombal**, embarked on reconstruction with grand squares that characterise parts of the city today. But as he accumulated more power, he became dictatorial, and following an assassination attempt on King **José I** he ordered mass arrests, expelling the Jesuits. It was only when **Maria I** came to the throne in 1777 that the Marquis was stripped of all his offices. In 1807 Napoleon's troops entered Lisbon, and in the Peninsular War, the English and Portuguese armies were victorious at the Battle of Buçaco in 1811. The queen had gone into exile in Brazil, and in 1820 while under a British governor, a new constitution was drawn up by a group of officers, giving universal male suffrage. By that time, Brazil had become a kingdom unified with the kingdom of Portugal. King **João VI** returned leaving his son **Pedro** as king of Brazil. This caused a succession crisis when João died in 1826. Pedro tried to abdicate in favour of his daughter, **Maria II**, but his brother **Miguel** immediately revolted and had to be defeated by forces from Britain, Spain and France in 1834. Although Portugal modernised in infrastructure and public health under Maria and her German husband **Ferdinand**, and their son **Pedro V**, Brazil and other territories had already been lost and the country was in a long decline. The rise of Liberalism and severe economic crises caused frictions with the royal family, who never accepted constitutional monarchy. The assassination of **Carlos I** and his heir Prince **Luis Filipe** in 1908 meant that the reign of **Manuel II** got off to a rocky start, and he was overthrown in the Revolution of October 5th 1910.

The First Republic inherited all of the political instability and perilous economics, which produced a succession of overthrows, bombings, and then a dictatorship in 1926. Into this government as Finance Minister in 1928 came António de Oliveira Salazar, an economics professor at Coimbra University. He had briefly held that position before, but resigned, and turned down repeated requests to rejoin the government until his demands for an iron hand in all spending were agreed to. He became Prime Minister in 1932, by which time he had produced budget surpluses, and initiated a programme of public works that eventually included the 25th April suspension bridge across the Tagus originally named after him. Hard to categorise, the *Estado Novo* – new state – under Salazar's leadership developed a highly authoritarian interpretation of Catholic social doctrine, which drew support from the Church in Portugal despite it being unable to wield political influence. Suppression of free speech and political parties included the Nazi-sympathising Syndicalists as well as Communists, Socialists and Liberals. Salazar's government lent help to the Nationalists during the Spanish Civil War as they did not want to see Socialism spread, and like Franco's Spain, Portugal remained neutral in World War Two but it was more about self-preservation, as Spain was close to the Axis powers. Portugal did, however, allow Allied use of facilities in the Azores, and accepted large numbers of refugees. Portugal had tried to expand inland from its bases in Africa, but that led to armed conflicts and increasing

candles should plan their dinner promptly and arrive early. Candles with plastic wind guards are on sale in all of the souvenir shops outside the Sanctuary.

On a plinth to the left of the chapel's entrance, exactly where the holm oak tree on which Our Lady appeared to the little shepherds used to be, is the **STATUE OF OUR LADY OF THE ROSARY OF FÁTIMA** (see also p. 15). The **crown** was donated by the women of Portugal in 1942. Fashioned at a leading Lisbon jeweller, it is made of gold and inlaid with pearls and precious stones; the bullet given by John Paul II is mounted below the orb – but on non anniversary/Feast days the original is on display in the Museum. The statue is often surrounded by a protective clear case. A slot in the plinth directly beneath the statue is for prayer requests, placed there by the custodians.

Next to the chapel, the **LARGE HOLM OAK TREE** is located. Here is where on May 13th 1917, thinking there was a storm brewing, the little shepherds had got to with their flock when they saw a second flash of lightning, just before they saw Our Lady for the first time. Before subsequent apparitions, they would pray the rosary under its shelter with people who had come along to witness or ask for help. Surrounded by a low wall, fence and a hedge, it is the only survivor in this part of the Cova from a century ago. Just behind, under the end of the north colonnade is the **PROJECTION ROOM** where several different films about Fátima are shown. Large groups should make a prior reservation at the Information Office.

Across from here in the centre of the Prayer area, is the **MONUMENT TO THE SACRED HEART OF JESUS and SPRING**. The bronze statue on a column on top of the earlier fountain house dates back to 1932. It symbolises the central place of Christ in the message of Fátima. Here is where you can also take the water of Fátima from the taps surrounding the monument. In 1921 the Bishop had ordered the digging to find water, when he learned that pilgrims and villagers did not have enough to go around. On November 9th the workers

Towards the Monument, Spring & Basilica of the Holy Trinity

dug deep, had hit rock and wanted to blast it, but the water suddenly appeared as if of its own accord. Many pilgrims have sought cures from the water on this spot, and many say they feel blessed when taking it. It is not necessarily held to be holy water, and as such, not all priests endorse it.

Stretching from the Basilica of the Most Holy Trinity down the slope to the Capelinha, **THE PENITENTIAL WAY** is a paved path for pilgrims who wish to make the last part of their journey on their knees, finishing on a loop around the Capelhina and alongside the Statue. It follows the path taken by Lúcia and her family in thanks to Our Lady for curing her mother (see p. 14). On a board is a prayer before making the 'pilgrimage on the knees'. You can walk across while pilgrims are making their way along it, but be respectful and allow them a little space.

Behind the *Capelinha* is the **HOUSE OF OUR LADY OF DOLORES (Sorrows)** which receives the sick during great pilgrimages and also serves as a retreat house for pilgrims in general. There is an array of facilities for these pilgrims, including refectory, meeting rooms and chapels. At the front of the complex, First Aid and a Doctor are available to all, and there is a breast feeding area. To the left is the **INFORMATION OFFICE** (see p. 40-41) where volunteers and employees will answer your specific questions; once answered you will not be ushered away, and it can be quite easy to get into a wider conversation with whoever you are speaking to if there is something on your mind. Next to it, we find the **PYRE**. Wax votives and candles of various sizes can be purchased here or beforehand from the shops, then join the queue, and you can usually put them in the pyre yourself.

Thus far, all the places described are in roughly the same area. Where you go next depends on what you want to do: perhaps you have a Mass to attend, or a meeting of your group. We are now going to cross over the other side of the *Recinto* on our way to the older Basilica.

Here, we approach the **RECTORY** of the Sanctuary and the administration offices, and just to its left is a **NATIVITY SCENE**. This is sculpted out of perforated stainless steel plate by local artist José Aurélio and was in place for the Great Jubilee of the Year 2000. The piece is triangular in form representing the Holy Trinity. At the top of the steps above is the **Chapel of the Angel of Peace**. Above and behind the Rectory is another retreat house complex - **OUR LADY OF CARMEL** - with similar array of facilities for visiting pilgrims.

We climb the steps on the right side **COLONNADE**. Built by António Lino, it is made up of 200 columns and half columns. There are 14 Stations of the Cross, each with a mosaic panel and altar. Above the Colonnade are 17 statues of saints: the four largest are Portuguese, including St Anthony of Padua; St Teresa of Ávila, St Ignatius of Loyola and St Simon Stock are among the others. Before we reach the top, pass the platform with a high canopy that at the great masses holds an altar and the celebrant. In the past temporary structures have been in place. At these large events there is usually a giant TV screen erected for those near the back of the Prayer Area to be able to see the ceremony close up.

BASILICA OF OUR LADY OF THE ROSARY

The Basilica is situated at the place where the children were playing on May 13th 1917 when they saw the first flash of lightning. Made of local limestone, it was designed by Dutch-born architect Gerardus Samuel van Krieken and continued by João Antunes. Begun in 1928, it was dedicated on October 7th 1953, and made a Basilica by Pope Pius XII on November 11th 1954. It was restored in time for the Centenary of the apparitions.

Most prominent is the 65 metre high **bell tower**, which is topped by a golden crown - made of bronze and later gilded - and a cross, illuminated at night. There is a carillon of 62 bells cast at a foundry in Fátima. In a niche is a **statue of the Immaculate Heart of Mary**. It was sculpted in Italy by the Dominican Fr Thomas McGlynn O.P. from the USA and blessed on May 13th 1958. He was faithful to his collaboration with Sr Lúcia, who described in detail how Our Lady appeared to her, and as such it is considered a more accurate

Inside the Basilica of Our Lady of the Rosary

likeness than the statue at the *Capelinha*. Above the statue is the first of a series of mosaics made in the Vatican workshops, this with the monogram NSRF – Our Lady (*Nossa Senhora*) of the Rosary Fátima.

Inside, the 14 bas-reliefs of the **side altars** are dedicated to the mysteries of the Rosary, while their stained glass windows represent invocations of the Litany of Our Lady; the 15th mystery is to be found in the chancel. In the four corners are **statues** of the saints known as the great apostles of the Rosary and of devotion to the Immaculate Heart of Mary: St Anthony Mary Claret, St Dominic of Gusman, St John Eudes and St Stephen – king of Hungary. Other windows depict **scenes of the apparitions**. The **arch** before the chancel is inlaid with a mosaic, a gift from the Catholics of Singapore; its inscription reads *Regina Sacratissimi Rosarii Fatimae Ora Pro Nobis* (Queen of the Most Holy Rosary of Fátima, pray for us). The main **altar** contains a Last Supper scene in silver. The large **painting** in the altarpiece is by João de Sousa Araújo and represents the Message of Our Lady which descends in the form of light and peace to meet the seers, with the Angel of Portugal having prepared them through their encounter with Christ in the Eucharist. The statue to the left of the altar is the first of the so-called **Pilgrim Statues** that have travelled the world. By José Ferreira Thedim, the same sculptor as the Statue of Our Lady, it is again collaboration with Lúcia, and so again is closer to her recollection; it was crowned on May 13th 1947. The **tomb of Bishop Alves** is also in the chancel.

In the transept are the **tombs of the seers**. Francisco is buried in the transept's right arm. The statue is by José Rodrigues and included are many birds, his favourite animals, and a lamb. The left arm contains the tombs of Jacinta and, since 2006, Lúcia. Jacinta was laid here on May 1st 1951 and Francisco on March 13th 1952. The artwork above their tombs depicts a shepherdess in the fields holding a lamb.

The **organ** was built in 1952 and, following a few years of silence, was rebuilt and inaugurated in March 2016. It is the largest in Portugal. **St Joseph's chapel** can be accessed either from the Sacristy or an outside door on the left. It is where marriages and baptisms are celebrated.

We now work our way back down the right side of the Recinto (our left) on our way to the newer Basilica and complex. On our way, by an entrance, is a slab of the **BERLIN WALL**. It is a significant reminder of the eventual fall of Communism in Russia, as the third apparition of Our Lady had foretold. After World War Two the Soviet Union had spread its sphere of influence to the Eastern European countries it had occupied by 1945, all of which set up Communist regimes. As Russian forces were first into Berlin, they continued their occupation of the east of the city. Eventually, in 1961, the Communist East German authorities built the wall to prevent people escaping to the free West. No symbol was more potent of the collapse of the Soviet system in 1989-90 than the destruction by euphoric re-unified Berliners of parts of the hated wall. This section was placed here in 1994. And, as we approach the Basilica, officially in John Paul II square, greeting us is a **STATUE OF SAINT JOHN PAUL II**. The statue is often adorned with flowers and votives from pilgrims. Next to it is the modern **High Cross**, 34 metres high and made of corten steel. The second **statue** is of **Pope Paul VI** the first pope to visit Fátima, in May 1967 on the 50th anniversary.

FÁTIMA AND THE WORLD

Devotion to Our Lady of the Rosary of Fátima has spread across the five continents. About 1,000 churches and chapels have been dedicated, as have several dioceses, associations, Consecrated Life, Missions and places of education. More than 250 sanctuaries exist.

The Pilgrim Statue that we see in the chancel travelled on its first mission in 1947. In 1945 a parish priest in Berlin had made the suggestion that a statue of Our Lady should visit all the capitals and Episcopal cities of immediate post-war Europe up to the border with Russia. The idea grew and such is the number of requests from all over the world for the statue to visit, that 13 replicas have been made. Reports are received from all corners of the reception afforded the statues, the people whose lives they touch and the pastoral harvest they yield.

BASILICA OF THE MOST HOLY TRINITY

As Fátima became more and more recognised, welcoming visitors from all over the world and the shrine forging links beyond the Catholic Church, the lack of capacity on many days became apparent. It was decided to build a new church and an international competition was launched in 1997, won by Greek architect Alexandros Tombazis. His plan at the opposite end of the Recinto was for an entirely circular structure 125 metres in diameter, yet only 21.5 metres in height at the maximum elevation of the roof. It can, therefore, take some time to realise how vast the internal space is when one enters, and lacking a cruciform with no decoration before reaching the chancel, the concept is decidedly modern. Sloping down and arranged as in an auditorium, there are no less than 8,633 seats. It can be divided into two distinct areas. The chancel holds 100 concelebrants, fully deployed during communion. The church was dedicated on October 12th 2007 at the 90th anniversary of the apparitions, and granted the title Basilica on June 19th 2012. Its dedication to the Holy Trinity reflects several themes: The Angel's repeated teaching the children its adoration; John Paul II who gave thanks to the Holy Trinity on his pilgrimage in 1982; The Jubilee Year 2000 was dedicated to the Holy Trinity – four years before the placing of the first stone of the church.

Into the **altar**, made out of local stone, is inset a piece of marble from the tomb of St Peter. It reminds us again of the bond between Fátima and the Holy Father. The bronze **crucifix** above is 7.5 metres high, its depiction of Christ untraditional. By the Irish artist Catherine Greene, it is intended to convey that

Christ is still alive, ever present. Apparently, she did not embark on the project as a Christian herself, but left it as one. Perhaps the most striking aspect is the 50 metre wide **mosaic panel**, gold to symbolise the holiness and fidelity of God and to encourage worshippers to be open to beauty, communion and love. Its author is Fr Marko Ivan Rupnik SJ, a Slovenian who studied in Rome; the work was carried out by artists from eight countries and four Christian denominations. The **statue of Our Lady** is by Benedetto Pietrogrande in Italian marble. A young Mary in a gesture of welcome shows her Immaculate Heart and the Rosary.

It might be best to view the exterior features when exiting the building. The **main door** is in bronze and dedicated to Christ, and next to it are 20 **panels** representing the mysteries of the Rosary. All are by Pedro Calapez. Below the panels are **two glass panels** with four biblical quotes, engraved in twenty-six languages. The **side doors** represent the 12 Apostles. Not to everybody's taste - even shunned by some Portuguese pilgrims who have been coming here for years - the Basilica of the Most Holy Trinity is deliberately international in outlook, welcoming to all, whilst faithfully presenting the tenets of the Fátima message. Its addition affirms the Sanctuary's worldwide importance as a place of pilgrimage, and its aim to embrace the widest spectrum of spirituality.

Either side of the Basilica - stairs on one side and ramps on the other - is

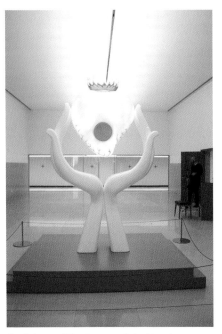

Sculpture of the Immaculate Heart

the complex of subterranean chapels and exhibition halls built at the same time. **The Galilee of Sts Peter and Paul** is the connecting corridor. The **chapel of the Blessed Sacrament** – or Adoration Chapel – is where the Blessed Sacrament is nowadays exposed. It is available 24 hours a day; the silver monstrance is set into the wall, and was designed by Zulmiro de Carvalho in 1986. The chapel has 200 seats. The **chapels of the Death of Jesus** and **of the Resurrection** are where masses are held and **confessions** heard – in both cases usually in Portuguese as the masses in other languages are most often in the chapel of the Apparitions. The chapels of the **Reconciliation** are where **confessions** are mostly heard, with **English always available**. They are separately dedicated to the **Sacred Heart of Jesus** and the **Immaculate Heart of Mary** and have respectively 16 and 12 confessionals. They are open from 7.30AM to 7.30PM without closing on Saturday and Sunday but closed from 1-2 Monday to Friday. The area is supervised unobtrusively; there are electronic boards giving the name of each priest, his availability, and the languages in which he can hear confessions.

The Pyre

There is also an **exhibition** space along this corridor which often hosts temporary displays.

Behind the Basilica, in Pius XII Square are **statues** of two more figures with strong associations with Fátima: wartime **Pope Pius XII**, and **Bishop José Alves Correia da Silva**.

Fatima Sanctuary

1 Chapel of the Apparitions and Statue of the Virgin
2 Large Holm Oak
3 Monument and Spring
4 Information Office
5 Pyre
6 Crucifix Sculpture
7 To Chapels – Confessions, Blessed Sacrament
8 Rectory
9 Retreat House of Our Lady of Carmel
10 Penitential Way

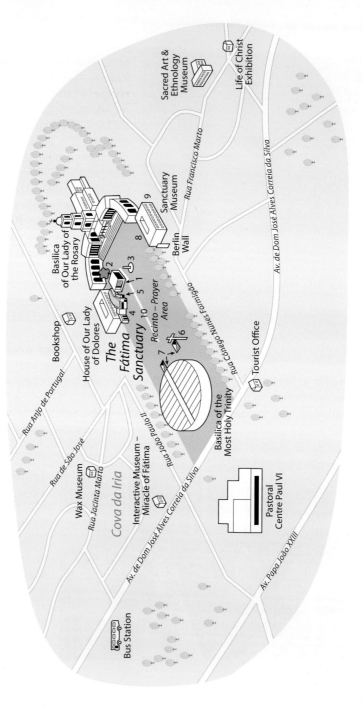

CLOSE TO THE SANCTUARY

Behind Pius XII square and a nowadays pedestrianised walkway that is part of Avenida D. José Alves Correia da Silva, there is another substantial modern complex. The **Pastoral Centre Paul VI** was begun in 1979 and inaugurated by John Paul II on May 13 1982. It has a large auditorium with 2,124 seats where concerts and performances of original plays and ballets are regularly held – look out for these. There is a smaller auditorium seating 800, several meeting rooms and a chapel. Various congresses are held here; in recent years Fátima has hosted a series of annual conferences on Marian pilgrimage. Also along the same street right ahead is the **Tourist Office** run by the Centro Portugal tourism region. Adjacent is the **Interactive Museum O Milagre de Fátima** which tells the story of the apparitions and the traditions of the shrine using modern multimedia, and further along the **Bus Station**. Not far away, on Rua Jacinta Marto, the **Wax Museum** (*Museu de Cera*) is another chance to learn the story of Fátima, with montages of the apparitions, John Paul II and Lúcia in later life.

By the northwestern entrance to the Sanctuary is a square containing the **Bookshop** - *Livraria*. It stocks the publications of the Sanctuary – including the Memoirs of Sister Lúcia – as well as complementary books from other publishers and is divided in part into language sections, books in English being near the door. There are prayer cards and other items for sale. Behind is an area reserved for the Blessing of automobiles which takes place on Sundays and Holy Days at 12.45 and 5PM.

Inside the Retreat House of Our Lady of Carmel, behind the Rectory is the **MUSEUM**. It was established early on by Bishop da Silva to conserve the history of the shrine. Its purpose has been added to since then. The permanent exhibition is entitled **Fátima Light and Peace** and reminds us that the apparitions occurred during the dark days of World War One. Its treasures comprise many gifts presented to Fátima over the years that are not displayed elsewhere in the Sanctuary. Foremost among these are:- **The Crown**, the original, when it is not worn by the Statue of Our Lady - **The Irish Monstrance**, made in Dublin of gilded silver and presented in 1949 – The **English Chalice**, a gift in 1946 from a London pilgrim in thanks for the ending of the Blitz – an **Indo-Portuguese Christ**, from the 17th century.

Open Tuesday to Saturday: 9AM - 12PM and 2.30 – 5.30PM; Sunday closes at 4.30PM; 13th of the month May-October closed in the morning; closed from December 24th afternoon and reopening January 2nd. Entrance: €1.

SANCTUARY INFORMATION A-Z

ADDRESSES

Main address:

Santuário de Nossa Senhora do Rosário de Fátima,
Apartado 31 2496-908 Fátima, Tel. **+351 249 539 600**
info@fatima.pt
www.fatima.pt

Rectorate: **reitoria@fatima.pt**
Pilgrims' Department: **sepe@fatima.pt**
Help in the preparation of pilgrimages and visits, incl. booking of chapels.
Pastoral care of the sick: **sedo@fatima.pt**
Lodging Department: **seal@fatima.pt**
Group or individual accommodation in the Sanctuary.
Liturgical pastoral Department: **sepali@fatima.pt**
Study and diffusion of the Fátima message: **estudos@fatima.pt**
Bookshop: **livraria@fatima.pt**
Religious articles shop: **artrel@fatima.pt**

ANNIVERSARIES

Each of the anniversaries of the apparitions of Our Lady is celebrated every year, but in particular the first and last, May 13th and October 13th with a great candlelight procession the evening before and a great Mass in the Recinto in the morning. As this book goes to press, Fátima celebrates the centenary of the apparitions, including the visit of Pope Francis on 12-13 May and the canonization of Blesseds Francisco and Jacinta Marto. Their Feast day is February 20th. You can expect additional celebrations on Feast days that are Portuguese national holidays (see p. 128).

BLESSINGS

The blessing of the sick takes place in a special area during each Eucharistic celebration on each anniversary day, May 13th to October 13th. Fátima also celebrates a Day of the Sick on February 11th with its own programme. Meet at First Aid point in front of the House of Our Lady of Dolores.

The blessing of religious objects is carried out each day at the end of the mass celebrations

The blessing of automobiles is carried out in the car park behind the bookshop (*Livraria*) every Sunday and Holy Day at 12.45 and 5.00PM (excepting Good Friday and when May 13th and October 13th falls on a Sunday).

PRAYER REQUESTS pedidos@fatima.pt

PUBLICATIONS *Voz da Fátima* Free monthly magazine, produced since 1922. Portuguese only.

'Fátima Light and Peace' is a quarterly newspaper, published in seven languages.

Subscription requests: **assinaturas@fatima.pt**

(state language for 'Fátima Light and Peace')

WALKING TO FÁTIMA

While the vast majority arrive by car or bus, organised groups from all over Portugal make the pilgrimage on foot. Pilgrims are received at the House of Our Lady of Dolores and given free dorm / tent accommodation and meal. If walking the Caminho de Santiago, it is possible to make a detour to Fátima. The two caminhos combine in some locations, including Santarém, and can be walked from the latter (55Km) in two days or from Tomar (27Km) in a day. There can be a lot of road walking involved; do your research beforehand. In other locations there are welcome links to both, such as at Estoril and Cascais.

Exhibits from the Museum

Part 5
TO ALJUSTREL VIA THE WAY OF THE CROSS

The Way of the Cross to the village of Aljustrel allows pilgrims to see the other significant sites of the apparitions, and where the children were born and lived, while as in the Rosary, we are presented with 15 incidents in the life of Jesus. All can be accomplished in a morning or an afternoon. Whether Lúcia ever consulted Google Street View this author has not researched, however you can follow the Way on that as part of your pre-trip research. The start is by the south roundabout – **Rotunda Sul** – on the way out of the town. It takes 10 minutes' walk from the Sanctuary, if going along Rua Francisco Marto: when you get to the huge *Rotunda* with the **statues** of the children in its midst, it is by the second road entrance anticlockwise; or if you have a tour bus it might take you there as a group – there is a lay-by right next to the start where you can disembark. Then it is roughly two Km to Aljustrel and two Km back. The Way itself is mostly flat alongside olive groves, beautifully maintained, and peaceful – it gives a sense of how the land at the Cova da Iria was used. There are toilets with washrooms, and the low walls alongside the path afford seating at any time; shade is not impossible to come by. The Way to Aljustrel and the visits should not be timed; however, if walking back from the house of Francisco and Jacinta, it is 15 minutes to the roundabout and therefore 25 minutes to the Sanctuary – a different route from the Way is recommended. Tour buses do pick pilgrims up in the village, clogging up the very narrow streets. There is also a good size car park in the village street mid way between the seers' houses.

The **Way of the Cross** is also known as the Little Shepherds' Way - *O Caminho dos Pastorinhos* - as it was the path taken by Lúcia, Francisco and Jacinta from their homes to the Cova da Iria. It was laid out between 1959 and 1962, and celebrates the connection between St Stephen of Hungary and the message of Fátima in the dedication of his kingdom to the Immaculate Heart of Mary. The **Hungarian chapel of St Stephen**, a gift from the Catholics of Hungary, is at the 14th and 15th Stations. The latter station was only inaugurated in 1992 as a gift from the parish of Lajosmizse in thanks for the 'resurrection' of their country two years after the fall of Communism in Europe.

The architect of the chapel and the stations is Ladislau Marec; the chapel stained glass and ceiling mosaics are by Peter Prokop. The bas-relief panels of the stations - many gifted by Hungarian congregations in the USA - and the statue of Our Lady Patroness of Hungary inside the chapel are by Maria Amélia Carvalheira da Silva. On the chapel roof is the **Hungarian Calvary**. The Group is by Domingos Soares Branco.

Hungarian Calvary

THE WAY OF THE CROSS

There is a plaque at each station giving a quotation from Sr Lúcia's Memoirs – at time of writing only in Portuguese. Here we shall concentrate on quotations from scripture, and St Alphonsus de Ligouri's suggestions for meditation. Our prayer will be to relate to Jesus' suffering for us as individuals and a world community.

JESUS IS CONDEMNED TO DEATH   1st Station

John 19:5-6

Jesus came out wearing a crown of thorns and the purple robe. Pilate said 'Here is the man.'

When they saw Him the chief priests and guards shouted 'Crucify Him, Crucify Him.'

Pilate said 'Take him yourselves and crucify him: I can find no case against him.'

Consider how Jesus, after having been scourged and crowned with thorns, was unjustly condemned by Pilate to die on the cross.

JESUS RECEIVES THE CROSS   2nd Station

John 19:11 'You would have no power over me,' said Jesus, 'if it had not been given you from above.'

10:17-18 'The Father loves me because I lay down my life in order to take it up again. No one takes it from me, I lay it down of my own free will.'

Consider how Jesus in making this journey with the cross on His shoulders, thought of us and offered for us to his Father the death He was about to undergo.

JESUS FALLS THE FIRST TIME 3rd Station

John 1:14 The word was made flesh, he lived among us.

1Cor. 1:25 God's weakness is stronger than human strength.
Consider this first fall of Jesus under his cross. His flesh was torn by the scourges, his head was crowned with thorns, and he had lost a great quantity of blood. So weakened he could scarcely walk and yet he had to carry this great load upon his shoulders. The soldiers struck him rudely, and he fell several times.

JESUS IS MET BY HIS MOTHER 4th Station

Luke 2:34-35 Simeon blessed them and said to Mary, his mother, 'You see this child: he is destined for the fall and for the rising of many . . . and a sword will pierce your own soul too.'

Consider this meeting of the Son and the Mother which took place on this journey. Their looks become like so many arrows to wound those hearts which loved each other so tenderly.

THE CROSS IS LAID UPON SIMON OF CYRENE 5th Station

Mark 15:21 They enlisted a passer-by, Simon of Cyrene, father of Alexander and Rufus, who was coming in from the country, to carry his cross.

Consider how the Jews, seeing that at each step Jesus was on the point of expiring, and fearing he would die on the way, whereas they wished him to die the shameful death of the cross, constrained Simon of Cyrene to carry the cross behind our Lord.

VERONICA WIPES THE FACE OF JESUS

6th Station

Mat. 25:36 'I was sick and you visited me, in prison and you came to see me.'

25:40 'I tell you solemnly, insofar as you did this to one of the least of these brothers of mine, you did it to me.'

Consider how the holy woman named Veronica, seeing Jesus so ill-used, and his face bathed in sweat and blood, wiped his face with a towel on which was left the impression of his holy countenance.

JESUS FALLS THE SECOND TIME

7th Station

Mark 14:35 'My soul is sorrowful to the point of death . . . he fell to the ground and prayed that, if it were possible, this hour might pass him by . . . let it be as you, not I, would have it.'

Consider this second fall of Jesus under the cross, a fall which renews the pain of all the wounds of his head and members.

THE WOMEN OF JERUSALEM MOURN FOR OUR LORD

8th Station

Luke 23:27-31 Large numbers of people followed him, and of women too, who mourned and lamented for him. But Jesus turned to them and said, 'Daughters of Jerusalem, do not weep for me, weep rather for yourselves and for your children. For the days will surely come when people will say "Happy are those who are barren, the wombs that have never borne, the breasts that have never suckled." Then they will begin to say to the mountains "Fall on us!" to the hills "Cover us!" For if men use the green wood like this what will happen when it is dry?'

Consider how those women wept with compassion at seeing Jesus in such a pitiable state, streaming with blood as he walked along.

JESUS FALLS THE THIRD TIME

Luke 22:56-61 As he was sitting there by the blaze, a servant girl saw him, peered at him and said, 'This person was with him too.' But he denied it. 'Woman,' he said, 'I do not know him.' Shortly afterwards someone else saw him and said, 'You are another of them.'But Peter replied, 'I am not, my friend.'

About an hour later another man insisted, saying 'this fellow was certainly with him. Why, he is a Galilean.''My friend,' said Peter, 'I do not know what you are talking about.' At that instant . . . the cock crew . . . and Peter remembered.

Consider the third fall of Jesus Christ. His weakness was extreme, and the cruelty of his executioners excessive who tried to hasten his steps when he could scarcely move.

JESUS IS STRIPPED OF HIS GARMENTS

10th Station

John 19:23-24 They took his clothing and divided it into four shares, one for each soldier. His undergarment was seamless, woven into one piece from neck to hem; so they said to one another, 'Instead of tearing it, let's throw dice to decide who is to have it.' In this way the words of the scripture were fulfilled:

Ps. 22:18'They shared out my clothing amongst them. They cast lots for my clothes. This is exactly what the soldiers did.'

Consider the violence with which Jesus was stripped by the executioners. His inner garments adhered to his flesh, and they dragged them off so roughly that the skin came with them.

JESUS IS NAILED TO THE CROSS

11th Station

Luke 23:33-34 When they came to the place called The Skull they crucified him there and the two criminals also, one on the right, the other on the left. Jesus said, 'Father forgive them; they do not know what they are doing.'

Consider how Jesus having been placed on the cross, extended his hands and offered to his eternal Father the sacrifice of his life for our salvation. Those barbarians fastened him with nails, and then securing the cross, allowed him to die with anguish on this infamous gibbet.

JESUS DIES ON THE CROSS

12th Station

Luke 23:44-46 It was now about the sixth hour and, with the sun eclipsed, a darkness came over the whole land until the ninth hour. The veil of the Temple was torn right down the middle, and when Jesus had cried out in a loud voice, he said 'Father, into your hands I commit my spirit.' (Ps 31:5)

With these words he breathed his last.

Consider how Jesus being consumed with anguish after three hours agony on the cross, abandoned himself to the weight of his body, bowed his head and died.

JESUS IS TAKEN DOWN FROM THE CROSS

13th Station

Luke 23:51-54 Joseph of Arimathaea went to Pilate and asked for the body of Jesus. He took it down, wrapped it in a shroud and put him in a tomb which was hewn in stone in which no one had yet been laid. It was Preparation Day and the sabbath was imminent.

Consider how after our Lord had expired, two of his disciples, Joseph and Nicodemus, took him down from the cross and placed him in the arms of his afflicted Mother, who received him with unutterable tenderness and pressed him to her bosom.

JESUS IS LAID IN THE SEPULCHRE

14th Station

Luke 23:55-56 Meanwhile the women who had come from Galilee with Jesus were following behind.They took note of the tomb and of the position of the body. They then returned and prepared spices and ointments. And on the sabbath day they rested, as the Law required.

Consider how the disciples, accompanied by His holy Mother, carried the body of Jesus to bury it; they closed the tomb and all came sorrowfully away.

HE HAS RISEN

Luke 24:2 'The stone is rolled away from the tomb.'

Mat. 28:6 'He is not here, for He has risen, just as He said. Come, see the place where He was lying.'

This is, of course, the first intimation of Christ's resurrection.

VALINHOS

Between the 8th and 9th stations is the **place of the fourth apparition** of Our Lady on August 19th 1917, the only one that did not take place at the Cova da Iria on the 13th of the month. See p.10-11. The **statue** is by Maria Amélia Carvalheira da Silva and the cover is by António Lino – again made possible by donations from Hungarian Catholics.

LOCA DO CABEÇO

This is the place of the **first and third apparitions** of the Angel – where the Angel was distinguishable and interacted with the children. See p.4-5. A lot of the signage calls it Loca do Anjo. It is signposted from the Way of the Cross and is only a small detour – afterwards retrace your steps and on to the final stations and chapel. The rocks referred to in Lúcia's memoirs are here. The same sculptress made a **Group** depicting the Angel's appearance to the children, who are praying as they were taught.

ALJUSTREL

Now we walk a short distance down into the village, and after passing a line of souvenir shops and cafes, come to a junction and **Lúcia's House** is on the street to the right (l/h side). Before the house is an **Ethnographic museum** [Entrance: €1; Open 10.30AM – 1PM, 3PM – 7PM summer; closed Tuesday]. It once belonged to Lúcia's godmother and has artefacts from the time; it will give you more of an understanding of how rural life was lived in the early 20th century. Lúcia's house is little altered from the time of her departure to Porto aged 14. You can see where she slept, her parents and siblings rooms, and where the family cooked and ate. Outside are sheep pens, and then, to see the site of the **second apparition of the Angel**, proceed to the back garden. The **well of Arneiro** contains another statue Group of the children before the Angel, this time by Maria Irene Vilar. The well itself is covered over, but again, there is an air of tranquility this time among fig trees. Back towards the street entrance is an information office. Lúcia donated the house to the Sanctuary in 1981.

At the junction turn right and shortly you will come to **Francisco and Jacinta's House.** Very similar to Lúcia's house, the Marto family home

Francisco's bedroom

contains artefacts filling the hearth and bedrooms. It is right on the narrow main street and can often feel more crowded and rushed. That is a pity, as one of the bedrooms is where Francisco passed away. Both siblings received **visions of Our Lady** in this house. Try to make your own space and time if you can.

To return to Fátima, it is better not to go back along the Way in the opposite direction, and indeed, you don't have to. Turn left on leaving the Marto house and continue along the street. Keep left to avoid taking any right forks that lead in the wrong direction. You come out on the Santarém road – turn left to get to the south roundabout, passing a traditional **windmill** by the petrol station.

Fatima Parish

1 Basilica of Our Lady of the Rosary
2 Basilica of the Most Holy Trinity
3 Bus Station
4 Pastoral Centre Paul VI
5 Valinhos
6 Hungarian Calvary & Chapel
7 Loca do Cabeço

8 Lucia Santos's House
9 Well of Ameiro
10 Lucia Santos Museum
11 Francisco & Jacinta Marto's House
12 Fátima Parish Cemetery
13 Mother Church of Fátima

•¹ Station of the Way of the Cross

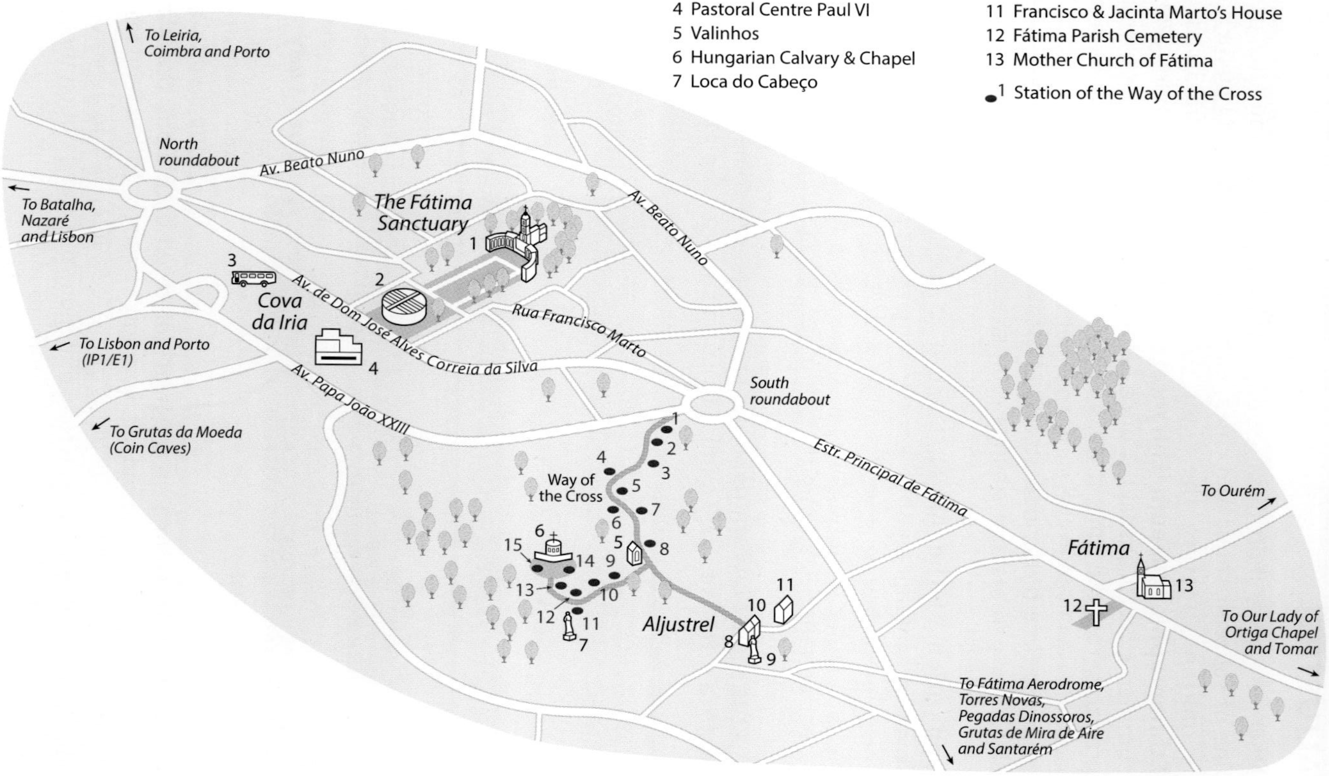

The Fátima Sanctuary

Cova da Iria

Way of the Cross

Aljustrel

Fátima

North roundabout

South roundabout

Av. Beato Nuno
Av. Beato Nuno
Rua Francisco Marto
Av. de Dom José Alves Correia da Silva
Av. Papa João XXIII
Estr. Principal de Fátima

To Leiria, Coimbra and Porto
To Batalha, Nazaré and Lisbon
To Lisbon and Porto (IP1/E1)
To Grutas da Moeda (Coin Caves)
To Ourém
To Our Lady of Ortiga Chapel and Tomar
To Fátima Aerodrome, Torres Novas, Pegadas Dinossoros, Grutas de Mira de Aire and Santarém

50

Part 6
FÁTIMA PARISH AND OURÉM

THE TOWN AROUND THE SANCTUARY

Besides the many hotels in all categories and **shops** selling religious articles, the sort of shops you would find in any town, banks, pharmacies and other services all abound. They include a couple of medium size supermarkets for those self-catering, and on the Santarém road (N360) a useful Chinese shop if you happen to lose or break a travel essential. Several **religious orders** have convents, seminaries and retreats here. In many cases, the retreats are for members or friends of the order, however, several do offer accommodation for pilgrims; some have opened full service hotels as well. In all, some 75 houses are present, the majority of them female religious.

We have featured the museums and exhibition spaces close to the Sanctuary. Two more museums not far away – along Rua Francisco Marto - should be mentioned. Run by the Consolata Fathers at their large complex, the **Sacred Art and Ethnology Museum** displays a collection of images of Jesus from the Nativity to the Passion, and missionary artefacts gathered from Portugal's former colonies. In addition, the **Shepherds Exhibition** features important articles from Francisco and Jacinta and their family. Open Tues – Sun 10AM-7PM (closes 5PM Nov - Mar). Entrance: €4.80 / Concessions for groups. Further along the road, the **Life of Christ** *(Vida de Christo)* is an impressive display of 33 scenes from the Annunciation to the Ascension, using 210 wax figures. Open Daily 9.30AM - 6.30PM. Entrance: €8.50.

We can now embark on a tour that takes in more sites associated with Fátima, together with an important local shrine, ending at the *Concelho* capital Ourém.

THE PARISH CHURCH

Here is where you can see the font from which the children were baptised, the Cemetery where Francisco was originally buried and Jacinta's body was placed after laying at Ourém and the Virgin to whom Lúcia prayed so diligently before and after the apparitions. The original parish centre is away - two Km southeast- from the town and Sanctuary: from the *Rotunda Sul* take the Ourém

/ Tomar road, the fourth exit if driving from the Sanctuary along Rua Francisco Marto. There is parking all around, but beware, this is a tricky junction.

The church in its present form dates back to the 16th century when it had only a single nave, with several subsequent modifications, including the bell

tower. Outside are **three statues** dating from 2000. Francisco is praying and Jacinta has her hand outstretched in a gesture of welcome. In between them resting on a tree trunk is a statue of Our Lady of Fátima. Inside, the **font** is in a tiled chamber to the left of the entrance. There are two **statues** inside the church on opposite side altars. Our Lady of the Rosary, to whom Lúcia prayed. The statue of Our Lady of Pleasures *(Nossa Senhora dos Prazeres)* is particularly fine. Removed from the Collegiate Church at Ourém in 1568, at the same time as the church here was elevated to the parochial church, it was hidden from plundering troops during the Peninsular War, and only uncovered during the renovations at the time of the apparitions.

Across the road, the Parish **Cemetery** has inside the gate, the mausoleum built when Jacinta's body was placed here in 1935, and where Francisco lay after his death in 1919. They were exhumed and reinterred in the Basilica of Our Lady of the Rosary.

SHRINE OF OUR LADY OF ORTIGA

Three Km further on, on the hill above the village of Casal de Santa Maria, there is the opportunity to visit a much older shrine than Fátima. Ortiga means nettles, and the statue is of Our Lady of Grace. The landscape, locality, and some aspects of the story are shared with the events at the Cova da Iria many years later.

The events are thought to have taken place in either the 14th or the 15th century. A shepherd girl, a deaf mute, was tending the family flock when suddenly Our Lady appeared to her above some nettle bushes. With a loving smile, the Lady asked the girl if she would give Her one of the lambs. Awestruck, the girl spoke for the first time in her life: 'I will have to ask permission of my father! Will you wait here?' The Lady agreed, and so the child ran off and burst into the house, explaining to her father what had happened and the request. Amazed that his daughter was speaking, he replied, 'Give Her whatever She wants!' The girl ran back. The Lady asked

The altar at Ortiga

the girl for a chapel to be built at the exact spot and vanished when her father arrived. As they were talking, father and daughter spotted something in the bushes, and retrieved the beautifully carved statue of the crowned Virgin and child. However, when the villagers heard the story, although they believed what had happened and were full of devotion, they decided to build the chapel in the village. They prepared their tools and materials and left them by the statue to retire for the night. The next morning, they discovered all had vanished; they found them back at the bushes, so they listened to the girl and built the chapel where Our Lady had appeared. In 1801 Pope Pius VII granted a Plenary Indulgence to all who visit the shrine on the **Feast day, July 1st**. Many thousands come annually. There are events up until July 3rd.

In the courtyard are a couple of traditional **windmills**. The **chapel** has stylised decorated roof, bell tower and porch – from restoration in the 1950s. In front of the entrance is a modern replacement cross with carved instruments of the Passion. Normally, entry is through the side. Inside, a plaque bears the pope's declaration. The statue rests in a Neoclassical altarpiece, flanked by images of St Vincent and St Catherine. Open: Morning to late afternoon.

Below Ortiga and bordering the Candeeiros Natural Park – is the village of **Casal do Farto**. It has a restored Gothic chapel that belonged to the Knights Templar, and some traditional houses, one with a 17th century sundial. Nearby are some old water cisterns.

OURÉM

It is only a short distance, turning north, to the *Concelho* capital. Ourém finally shed its Vila Nova tag in 1991. It is essentially in two sections: the original town was built around the impressive castle and palace high on a hill; the fertile valley below was settled once it became safe to do so. The well preserved **old town** is our next stop. The narrow streets inside the walls are a delight, and the views far-reaching. It served as an outpost of the castle at Leiria during the Reconquista. Later, a grateful King João I gave the county of Ourém to his general, **Nuno Álves Pereira** after the 14th century Battle of Aljubarrota. He later became a Carmelite friar, and was canonised as Saint Nuno of Saint Mary in 2009. The **castle** was remodelled in the 15th century by Count Afonso (Nuno's grandson) who built the **palace**, fortified along Italian lines. They were not fully rebuilt from the ravages of the Lisbon earthquake and the Peninsular War; the remains of both can viewed today. Aside from the castle complex, the main monument is the **Collegiate Church of Our Lady of Mercies** *(Misericórdias)* which was founded in 1445 and rebuilt after the earthquake. In its crypt is the tomb of the Count Afonso – one of the finest in Portugal. The **south gate** bears the coat of arms of King João IV and weapons of the town, while next to it is the **chapel of Our Lady of the Conception** (1642). There are several gastronomic specialities unique to the area. One of the most notable is a quality dessert wine – *Abafado* – and there is a revival of a medieval table wine – *Palheto* – which is 80% white and 20% red.

There are soups, sausages, cheese, lamb stew, cakes and puddings. One place to try a selection is in the restaurant of the old town's *Pousada* hotel.

We now move on to the **newer town**. The **church of Nossa Senhora da Piedade** (Praça da República – parking off the square - toilets) dates back to the 18th century. Inside, a Pietà is mounted above a side altar. Head northeast. At the square Largo Dr. Vitorino de Carvalho, a new **Municipal Museum** has opened on the site of the house of the former Administrator, Artur Santos. Here is where the children spent most of 13th to 15th August 1917. The museum gives insights into the life of the man vilified for his actions to disrupt the events at the Cova da Iria. Open Tues. – Sun. 9AM-1PM & 2-6PM; Entrance €2.50. Across the square, from an upstairs window of the **former hospital**, a picture of Jacinta looks down – this is where she was confined before being moved to Lisbon shortly before her death. The **cell** – or room - at the former jail where the children were first sent on August 15th is set to open in 2017.

Leave the town heading northeast turning right onto the N113 that is the main artery through it, and soon turn left onto the R349 up towards Olival. Not long afterwards, pull in to the car park outside the **Municipal Cemetery.** Here is where Jacinta's body was taken from Lisbon to the private mausoleum of Baron Alvaiázere, where it lay until 1935. It is another indication of the intense interest that some influential people were taking in the nascent pilgrimage while it was still officially banned. During the translation to the cemetery at Fátima, the body was found to be incorrupt. There is a **memorial** to her here now, just inside the gate on the left.

In another eight minutes we reach the village of **Olival**. Above the village centre is the **church of Our Lady of the Purification**. Founded by the Templars and tended by the Cistercians - a curate of the Collegiate church at Ourém - the present structure dates from the 15th century with remodelling in the 17th and 18th centuries. The statue of Our Lady is housed in a gilded altarpiece, with chequered wall tiles by the side. Not always open. The tradition gave birth to a largely secular celebration of thanksgiving for the fruits of nature. Feast: first Saturday, Sunday and Monday in September.

Heading back out of the village but straight on/left at the traffic light (rather than r/back to Ourém) takes us through delightful countryside to **Caxarias** where another important shrine is kept open. It is round a sharp bend before the junction with the N356 and parking is possible on the chapel's own drive. **The chapel of Our Lady of the Conception** *(Conceição)* dates from 1578 and is in the Mannerist style. Surrounded by a porch, the chancel is clad in geometric tiles and has a decorated ceiling. The retablo houses the statue of the Virgin. Originally it was a place of healing, as there were mud baths that cured diseases including malaria. Feast: first weekend in May.

AIRE E CANDEEIROS NATURAL PARK AND THE COIN CAVES

In the southeast corner of the Ourém Concelho lie the mountains of the **Serra de Aire**. Together with the Serra de Candeeiros nearer to Alcobaça, and two large plateaux, they make up the **Natural Park of Aire e Candeeiros**. Where they are not bare limestone rock, the mountains are sparsely covered. Apart from the main attractions, it is good hiking and birdwatching country.

The caves are justly famous. In the town of **Mira de Aire**, the caves with their underground lake and waterfall are incorporated into a modern above-ground water park. From here, there are more caves off the N243 before **Alvados**. This road runs through the Park until it winds its way into **Porto de Mós**, an attractive medieval town that has a castle with green pointed turrets, the Baroque church **of São Pedro** and the **chapel of Santo António**.

The **Grutas da Moeda** (Coin caves) are further back from the Natural Park between Fátima and São Mamede, just minutes from the Sanctuary (leave via the north roundabout) and so can be visited separately if your pilgrimage programme allows. They are named after a legend, in which a man carrying a large bag of money was attacked by bandits and fell into a sinkhole, the coins scattering throughout the underground system. The caves were rediscovered in 1971. With 350 metres in length of visitable space, a series of galleries are appropriately named: Lake of Happiness, Nativity Scene, Shepherd's Room, Waterfall, Red Cupola, Flawed Chapel, Red Dome, and Spring of Tears. Open 9AM – 5PM Oct. to March, till 6PM April to June, & 7PM July to Sept.

The Natural Monument of the **Dinosaur Footprints** are at **Bairro** south of Ourém and southeast of Fátima (N360 / N357). The footprints were discovered in 1994 in a quarry - the Pedreiro do Galinha - and are from the Middle Jurassic period, making them about 175 million years old. There are 1,000 in total, coming from Sauropods – herbivores - laid out in a series of 20 tracks. Open Tues. to Sun. 10AM-12.30PM & 2PM-6PM; summer closing time 8PM weekends and public holidays. Entrance €3/Concessions, plus €1 for a guided tour.

Part 7
VISIT TO THE ABBEYS OF BATALHA AND ALCOBAÇA

The UNESCO World Heritage List contains no less than three historic religious monuments in Fátima's immediate surrounding area. A Combined ticket can be bought at the first site you visit for €15 – a €3 saving overall. Today's excursion includes two of them, and offers a full day's programme if all the stops are made, with an hour's travelling time each way. Take the N356 from the North roundabout. If time is shorter, then there is still not much to be saved by following the N357 and picking up the IC9 and exiting at the sign for Batalha – but missing out Reguengo do Fetal and its twisty valley.

REGUENGO DO FETAL – PROCESSION OF THE SNAILS

On the way from Fátima to Batalha with the Serra de Aire to the left, the N356 winds down the steep valley, and then starts to climb its side. You will see **Stations of the Cross** on the right side of the road, donated by neighbouring parishes in devotion to what is now a 500-year-old pilgrimage tradition. The village centre is off left, then past the **parish church of Our Lady of the Remedies** *(Remedios)* head for the Cemetery climbing up through the narrow lanes. There are two large spaces opposite the Cemetery. One contains the tiny **Chapel** the other a shelter with a depiction in **tiles** *(azulejos)* of the miracle.

Legend has it that during a time of great famine in the area, when the people only had snails to eat, a shepherd girl was weeping as she looked at her emaciated flock. She was aware of a presence and, looking up saw the image of a Lady shining bright. 'Why are you weeping?' She asked. The girl explained, adding that the family had eaten their last piece of bread. 'Go home and ask your mother to give you some bread,' replied the Lady, and when the girl protested, the Lady repeated, and then vanished. So, the girl went home and when her mother opened the bread bin, there were bountiful supplies of fresh bread to feed the whole village. The villagers followed the girl to the spot in the hope that the Lady might also provide them with water, and there was uncovered a spring. Soon after, the rains came and the famine was over.

Feast day: 1st Sunday in October, all day also with Mass, procession and celebrations the night before. It is then that the people of the village pour olive oil into hundreds of snail shells and light wicks inside them to make lamps; they are placed on ledges and on the ground, making elaborate shapes, as an illuminated sign to the Lady in heaven. Also, there is an evening procession on the last Saturday of September, when the statue is transferred from the chapel to the parish church. The evening processions are also known as the **Procession of the Snails.**

THE ABBEY AT BATALHA

Now we arrive at one of the Gothic jewells of Europe. On the day of the Battle of Aljubarrota, August 14th 1385, João made a vow to the Virgin Mary – **Santa Maria da Vitória** – that he would build a great abbey if She would deliver him victory over the Spanish forces of Juan I and with it the throne of Portugal. The following year, work began at a site close to the battlefield, with the new town around it eventually christened 'Battle'. A community of several dozen Dominican friars were endowed to pray a perpetual Rosary to offer the thanks of Portugal for Our Lady's favours. The king also created a royal pantheon for the Avis dynasty to be buried.

João appointed master architect Afonso Domingues, an exponent of the Rayonnant Gothic style that, in reality at the time, was being superceded. Portugal needed to play catch-up and in 1402 Huguet took over as principal architect. It is theorised Huguet was from Catalonia, and it is likely that the Queen, Philippa of Lancaster was influential in his appointment. At this time, only parts of the church, transept and chapter house were complete. A proponent of both the flamboyant Gothic and the Perpendicular styles, Huguet was therefore able to stamp his much more adventurous approach on the work. He raised considerably the height of the nave to its present 32.5m and its groin vaults, using techniques in use at Westminster Abbey and Canterbury Cathedral. The death of King João (1433) and the succession of his son, Duarte, propelled the construction of a new pantheon around the choir, however Huguet's flourish of creativity was halted by the premature death of Duarte (1438) with the chapels unfinished. Only he and his queen, Eleanor of Aragon, are buried here, and only since 1940. A later 16th century initiative by King Manuel I and the architect Mateus Fernandes added the beautiful portal to the chapels – a high point of Manueline art - but the work stopped there, with the apse remaining open to the elements. In between times, King Alfonso V added a late 15th century second cloister, a much simpler affair. The Dominicans remained until 1834, when many religious orders were expelled and while services are held there today, the abbey is primarily a museum.

Perpendicular naves

The **main doorway** is Huguet's masterpiece, with Christ in Majesty flanked by the Four Evangelists who are busy writing the Gospels. The archivolts have various figures arranged according to celestial hierarchy, while the jambs have statues of the 12 Apostles. Once inside, the **central nave** shows the breathtaking scale and effect of the perpendicular style with a virtual wall of dense columns and a ribbed ceiling vault. To the right is the **Founder's Chapel**, the pantheon containing the tombs of João and Philippa, their carved figures lying hand-in-hand under an octagon. His four younger sons and their wives are in the recessed tombs, including under a baldachin, Henry the

Navigator. If you are going on to Burgos in Spain with its Gothic masterpiece of a cathedral, the design is so similar to the chapel of the Condestables – don't forget to pinpoint it when you get back outside. To the left is the **Cloister of King João I**, which displays the influences of both the original

Unfinished chapels through the Manueline portal

masters, with arcade screens added in a later semi-Manueline style. The **Chapter House** was begun by Afonso Domingues, but the single vaulted roof is by Huguet who managed not to use a central support. The 16th century stained glass depicts the Passion. The **Refectory** displays offerings to the **Unknown Soldier** - the guarded tomb holds the remains of two WWI casualties, one from Flanders and one from the African theatre. The **Alfonsine Cloister** is further off to the left, containing the cells of the Friars.

To reach the **Unfinished Chapels**, exit the complex and cross round the courtyard – where once there were two more cloisters. There are seven side chapels with vaulted ceilings leading off the central apse. You can climb a narrow flight of stairs up onto the roof from here, alongside the openwork tracery, to gain different perspectives of this magnificent work – May only be open to guided tours/groups.

Open Daily 9AM - 6.30PM April to October; closes at 5.30PM in winter. Closed 1st January, Easter Sunday, 1st May, Christmas Eve and Christmas Day. Admission €6; Concessions. Guided tours must be booked in advance. www.mosteirobatalha.pt

BATTLEFIELD OF ALJUBARROTA

Leaving Batalha, follow the IC2/EN1 southwest for a few minutes to **São Jorge**. **The Interpretation Centre for the Battle of Aljubarrota (CIBA)** is on the left. After touring the Centre, you can tour the site with the remains of the **trenches**, the **positions** of the Castilian and French, Portuguese and English, and the **chapel** dedicated to St George. The legend of the battle is that a baker woman beat the Spaniards with her bread shovel and pushed them into the oven. Open Tues. to Sun. 10AM – 5.30PM. Multimedia shows: 11.30AM, 3PM, 4.30PM. Admission €7; Concessions. Audiotour in English €3 (for 2 people).http://fundacao-aljubarrota.pt

ALCOBAÇA

Continue along the N8 for another 20 minutes, passing through Aljubarrota. Victory in battle also was the precursor to the next abbey we visit. It was the earlier reconquest of Santarém from the Moors in 1147 that prompted the recently crowned Afonso Henriques to build a church. The

king endowed it as a gift to the Cistercian reformer, St. Bernard of Clairvaux shortly before his death in 1153. The great Gothic church was completed in 1223, with King Dinis adding the cloister a century later, and further significant additions in the 16th, 17th and 18th centuries. Concentrating

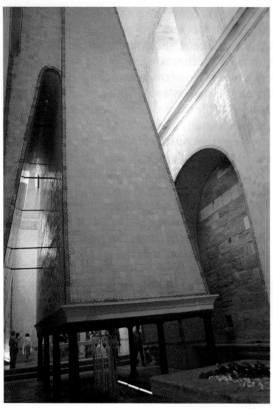
Kitchen

the present **Kitchen** is, despite all the other attractions, perhaps the most memorable. This is mainly for its enormous tiled chimney that sits on eight iron pillars – big enough to roast three oxen at once. The water basin, channel and outside traps allowed fish to be channelled in directly. The vaulted **Refectory** is fine of form, with its interesting pulpit from which a monk would read during the meal, approached by a staircase covered by interlocking arches. Since 1834 the monastery has had many alternative uses, with the Refectory serving as a public theatre.

Open Daily 9AM – 7PM April to September; closes at 6PM in winter. Closed 1st January, Easter Sunday, 1st May, 20th August and Christmas Day. Admission €6; Concessions. Free admission first Sunday in the month until 12Noon. Note: Individual Ticket must be purchased to visit the Sacristy - €2. www.mosteiroalcobaca.pt Guided visits – see website.

On the return journey, there is a possible detour to another Cistercian establishment, the **Convent of Santa Maria de Cós**. It was founded in 1279 by the Abbot of Alcobaça although the structure we see today is 16th – 17th century with a Baroque altarpiece, painted ceiling the length of the nave, and tiled sacristy.

Part 8
VISIT TO TOMAR AND THE CONVENT OF CHRIST

In this excursion we visit the third monastery in the vicinity of Fátima on the UNESCO World Heritage List. The medieval town of Tomar is a mere 30 minutes east of the Sanctuary if you actually start from the north roundabout, taking the N357 before joining the IC9. The extended Templar trail concludes with watery views from attractive towns and their famous castle at Almourol.

THE KNIGHTS TEMPLAR AND THE ORDER OF CHRIST

Cross of the Order of Christ - flag (Creative Commons) see also p.25

Several military orders played leading roles in the reconquest of the Iberian Peninsular. Tomar became the headquarters of the Knights Templar in Portugal. The order was founded by three Knights, Hugues de Payens, Andre de Montbard and Godfrey St-Omer in 1120 to protect pilgrims in the Holy Land on their journey from the port of Jaffa to Jerusalem. They were given lodgings at the Al-Aqsa Mosque on the Temple Mount, believed to be above Solomon's Temple. The knights themselves wore a white mantle – for purity – with a large red cross – symbolising their blood - across the breast. They lived frugally under a semi monastic rule and were highly skilled in warfare. The rule is believed by many to have been written by St Bernard of Clairvaux (de Montbard's nephew). In 1139 Pope Innocent II's papal Bull *Omne Datum Optimum* exempted the Templars from local laws, including border controls and taxes, and it quickly became the order to which nobles eager to fight for the Holy Land sent their sons or assigned over their lands while they embarked on a crusade. So, having initially relied on charity, the order developed into a powerful body with functions beyond the military, and even established an early banking system, building castles, cathedrals and monasteries. In 1139 King Afonso Henriques had donated the castle and lands at Cera along the banks of the Nabão river which the Moors had called Tomar, to the Templars. In 1147 they took part in the capture of Santarém and Lisbon. In 1190 in Tomar, the knights and townspeople, led by legendary Grand Master **Dom Gualdim Pais**, beat off an attack by the Emir of Morocco. By the end of the 12th century the Templars were protecting several important parts of the kingdom.

As the Muslim forces in the Middle East, including those of Saladin, became better organised, the Templars lost their holdings, and in 1307 were coerced by King Philip IV of France – who was heavily in debt to the order – into a series of false confessions on charges of heresy. Pope Clement V was forced first to order seizure of the Templars' assets, and then to disband the order. Their leaders were burned at the stake, but within a year both king and pope were dead and the persecution stopped. Some remnants of the order were absorbed into the Knights Hospitaller – the order of St John of Jerusalem – but in Portugal in 1319 they became the Order of Our Lord Jesus Christ – or simply the **Order of Christ** - under the patronage of King Dinis and the approval of Pope John XXII. One could term the latter Templar Mark II as it inherited all the former order's privileges and assets. Henry the Navigator became its Grand Master in 1417, as he used the order to prepare for the Voyages of Discovery: the knights who had fought to establish the Christian kingdom now setting out as his ships' captains in unmistakable symbolism. They were also permitted to marry so that they could populate the colonies. Henry also built up the town below the convent in the shape of a cross. Today the order is active in Portugal and Brazil – conferred on individuals for outstanding service - and in the Holy See there is the parallel Supreme Order of Christ – currently dormant.

The Templars are even today shrouded in mysticism. Much of this surrounds their earliest origins and the relics that the order is said to have discovered at the Temple Mount – the Ark of the Covenant, the Holy Grail, and the mummified head of John the Baptist – together with the eccentricities of their rule. The myths have been perpetuated in fiction, most recently in The Da Vinci Code. In Tomar, there are two locations that draw visitors fascinated by the Templar cult besides those who simply want to see unique architecture. But all around the region, there are many reminders of the influence of the Order of Christ.

THE CONVENT OF CHRIST

In a commanding position overlooking the attractive town, and today surrounded by gardens below, the Convent of Christ with its neighbouring **Castle**, is truly unique. From the **Porta do Sol** gate and the ticket office, we first pass alongside the **main Cloister**. Built under King João III by Diogo de Torralva and completed by Filipe Terzi, it is one of the best exemplars of the Renaissance style in Portugal. We then see **Prince Henry's two cloisters** – the 'Cemetery' and the 'Washing' cloisters.

The **Charola** is the original round Templar church built into the Castle, with its central octagon, in the characteristic style of the Dome of the Rock and the Holy Sepulchre. The church was only for the knights, and it is said that they attended Mass on horseback. The decoration is late Gothic and Manueline, Manuel I having opened up one end to add a nave and choir. His chapter house is famous for its **chapter window** by Diogo de Arruda – complete with every conceivable seafaring motif. This is best viewed from outside on the upper gallery of the St Barbara Cloister. The elaborate **portal is** by João de Castilho and was completed after Manuel's death, c. 1530.

The Charola viewed from the choir

The chapter window

In the 16th century, first João III and then the Spanish King Philip expanded the monastery to the west of the castle, building where the townspeople had previously lived. **Four more cloisters** were constructed together with an **aqueduct** with 180 arches stretching for six Km. Other parts of this great complex include the former **Infirmary** which only closed in 1993, and its **Pharmacy** – one of the earliest. The **Sete Montes Enclosure** is a harmonious garden space that was integral to the monastic life, and in grounds northeast of the convent, the Mannerist style **Chapel of OL of the Conception** is understood to have been designed as the final resting place of João III - although in the end he was buried at Jerónimos Monastery.

Open Daily 9AM – 6.30PM June to September; closes at 5.30PM at other times. Closed 1st January, Easter Sunday, 1st May and Christmas Day. Admission €6; Concessions. Free admission first Sunday in the month.

CHURCH OF SANTA MARIA DO OLIVAL

We find this 13th century Gothic church standing on its own on the opposite side of the town and river from the convent. It served two main purposes. It

was the Templars' Parish Church as opposed to the Charola that was reserved for the knights. However, its significance goes way beyond that. Built originally by order of Gualdim Pais, who is among the many knights buried here, it served initially as the mother church of the diocese for all of the lands of the Discoveries. The west

Templar church of Santa Maria do Olival

façade includes a lovely rose window – there is a smaller one on the east side – and an attractive portal with archivolts. However, the level of decoration has been kept to a minimum. There are two images of the Virgin and Child – OL of the Milk, and the Holy Mothers – and some decorative tiles from the later 16th century additions. The former watchtower serves as the belfry. Another of the myths is that a secret underground passage exists to connect the convent with the church, and that Templar treasure is buried either here or at the castle at Almourol.

AROUND THE PRAÇA DA REPÚBLICA

The historic centre of Tomar includes the attractive Manueline **Church of São João Baptista** in the main square. There is a flamboyant Gothic portal, and the interesting tower. The inner columns of the nave have decorated capitals, and some important 16th century painted panels are attributed to Gregório Lopes. Opposite the church is the **Town Hall** which was originally the royal residence of Manuel I before it was remodelled in the Mannerist style. Henry the Navigator encouraged the Jewish community in Tomar. Their **Synagogue** (Rua Dr Joaquim Jacinto – down from the Praça then left) is open 10AM– 7PM though no community survives. This building is mainly 16th century, and so would not have been the original. Incorporating the **Museum of Abraham Zacuto**, it has some interesting architectural detail and artefacts.

In the central park, one of the w**ater wheels** survives along with the waterside former mills and olive oil presses, which utilised the hydro power. **The Núcleo de Arte Contemporânea** (Travesa Gil de Avô) is a collection of Portuguese art from the mid 20th century onwards, assembled by an art professor and critic. Tomar's patron (and Santarém's) is 7th century Saint Irene – *Santa Iria* (Feast Day October 20th). Part of a convent, a **chapel** dedicated to her near to where she was martyred is located over the Ponte Velha on Rua Marquês de Pombal – but is generally open weekend afternoons. This route is the exit from Tomar on the **Caminho Portugués** – the increasingly popular Portugal walking pilgrimage to Santiago de Compostela to which it is a further 460Km. A modern Hostel (rua Serpa Pinto) has opened to cater mainly for pilgrims, supplementing Tomar's good collection of accommodation. Europe's largest private **matchbox collection** – *Museu dos Fósforos* (Av. Gen. Bernardo Faria, down towards the rail station) is located in the former convent of San Francisco. Closed Mondays.

The **Festival of the Trays / *Festas Dos Tabuleiros*** is one of the best known festivals in Portugal, renowned internationally, and takes place once every four years – the next being July 2019. Probably originally a pagan bread cult, once Christianised it was dedicated to the cult of the Empire of the Holy

Spirit in which infidels would unite in harmony with Christians. The stacks of bread each symbolised a pillar of the Temple of Jerusalem. Young girls dressed in white process through the town, each carrying a tray on her head stacked high with loaves and decorated with flowers. At the end of the festival, the bread is distributed to the poor along with meat and wine.

(Turismo Centro Portugal)

EAST OF TOMAR TO CASTELO DE ALMOUROL

There are several attractive spots overlooking water in two different directions, at either end of the **Castelo de Bode Dam** and along the **Zêzere and Tagus rivers**. Northeast, the town of **Dornes** was influenced by Queen Saint Isabel (Elizabeth) wife of King Dinis, who built a church there. The lake has made the town into a peninsular. The tower was built by the Templars as part of their commanderie.

At the other end of the lake and beyond, **Constância** is a beautiful white painted floral town, home of Portugal's most famous poet Luis de Camões. The **Igreja de Nossa Senhora dos Mártires** is the Mother church and stands at the top of the town. The **Igreja da Misericórdia** has a collection of 17th century tiles. The town also has a maritime museum and an astronomy centre, besides offering boat trips and hiking trails.

Further southeast of Tomar, we arrive at one of Portugal's most romantic settings. The **Castle at Almourol** stands on an island in the wide river Tagus. It is suggested that there was a Lusitanian fortress here originally, in which case the Romans took it over as there are remains of their walls and coins have been discovered. It was later occupied by the Visigoths and then the Moors. It was part of the land and assets donated by King Afonso Henriques to the Knights Templar, who substantially improved it in 1171 under Gualdim Pais, as part of a line of fortifications. The castle then passed to the Order of Christ. The quadrangular spaces and circular towers characteristic of Templar military architecture can be seen today, although the structure was 'romanticized' in the 19th century.

A great collection of **legends** surrounds the castle. One has it that the castle was once inhabited by a giant named Almourol, who guarded two young princesses, Miraguarda and Polinarda. An English knight named Palmeirim who had stopped at Porto on his way to the crusades, heard of the princesses and decided to go and win one of them. He fought the giant and escaped with Polinarda; however another version has it that he failed and Almourol was eventually defeated by another giant. Another is a tragic tale of the bloodthirsty Visigothic lord of the castle, Don Ramiro, who murdered the mother and sister of a Moorish boy and forced him to work as a page. The boy and the mayor's daughter, Beatriz, fell in love and ran away, causing the father to die of a broken heart. It is said the lovers appear on the keep on moonlit nights, including St John's Eve.

The castle can be visited on a trip by boat from **Tancos** or in front of the castle. Open 10AM-1PM & 2.30-7.30PM March to October; shorter hours in winter; closed Mondays October-April.

Inclusive price €2.50 - €4 depending on numbers of passengers.

Guided Tours: Tel. Tourist Office 249090405 or 915081737.

Beyond the castle, **Vila Nova da Barquinha** is another attractive town along the Tagus where one can enjoy fish from the river and sea. It is less than an hour's drive back to Fátima.

Part 9
VISIT TO SANTARÉM AND THE EUCHARISTIC MIRACLE

Many of the escorted pilgrimage tours that stay a little longer in Fátima make one or two excursions. One of the most popular is to historic Santarém to visit the Miraculous Host, which has found worldwide fame. Hopefully, once you have visited the Miracle in its own church, there will be time to explore at least some of the many monuments. Santarém, however, does have no less than two days on which most of the monuments are closed – Mondays and Tuesdays plus holidays. Nevertheless, you will normally be able to visit the Miracle – see Pilgrimage Information below– but for those who want to see more of the city, it is better to avoid these days if you can. Santarém by road is about 40 minutes' south of Fátima and about the same north of Lisbon, so as an alternative it can be visited on the way to a stay in Fátima. The express

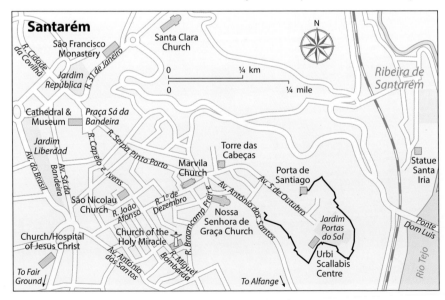

72

buses from Lisbon are frequent - as are the trains - whereas buses in each direction between Fátima (no rail station) and Santarém are infrequent -making a day trip from Lisbon a perfectly feasible alternative. A taxi is recommended upon arrival at either the bus or the rail station.

Occupying a strategic position high above the river Tagus *(Tejo)* Santarém has been populated since Neolithic times. After Roman conquest, Julius Caesar established a new fort and *Scallabis* became one of the principal settlements of the province of Lusitania. Excavations have revealed remains of a temple, podium, a theatre and baths. The Visigoths expelled the Alans, following which it was taken by the Moors. The conquest of Santarém in March 1147, preceding that of Lisbon in the same year, allowed King Afonso Henriques to consolidate his new kingdom. Santarém therefore became a favourite of royalty and although the palace is no longer, it is known as the capital of Portuguese Gothic. **Santa Iria** (Saint Irene) is the city's patroness, from whom its name is derived, after it is said that her incorrupt body floated down the river from Tomar where she had been martyred in 653. Her **statue** and **church** are down by the old river port - *Ribeira de Santarém* - and it is believed that should the waters ever rise to reach her feet, Lisbon will be deluged. The city on its own has a population of 30,000 and sees itself as an agricultural centre – so much so that the national **agricultural fair** is held every year at the beginning of June. Besides trade, there are folk events, horse races and bull running. A number of **stud farms**, specializing in Lusitanian horses, dot the area. In late October a big national **gastronomy festival** takes place with many food stalls. There is a dedicated **fair ground** on the southwest outskirts of the city.

THE HOLY MIRACLE OF SANTARÉM

In 1247, there lived in Santarém an unhappy woman, who was convinced that her husband was being unfaithful. Having tried to win back his affections, in desperation she turned to a sorceress. The sorceress promised the woman that her husband would love her as before, but she would have to bring her a consecrated Host instead of consuming it. Knowing this to be sacrilege, the woman nevertheless attended Communion at the church of St Stephen and took the wafer out of her mouth, hid it in her veil, and hurried out of the church. People the woman passed in the street asked her if she was alright as she appeared to be bleeding. She discovered that her veil was soaked in fresh blood, surrounding the Host, and perplexed, instead of re-visiting the sorceress, hurried home and hid the veil in a wooden chest. The woman did not tell her husband what had happened, not daring to look in the chest to see if the Host was still bleeding. That night, they were awoken by rays of light that burst out of the chest. Some versions of the account – there were documents that were re-read in the 15th century and then lost – state that the rays of light were accompanied by the music of angels, others that a vision of angels adoring the Holy Host was seen. The woman confessed her sin to her husband, who in turn confessed his, and both spent the rest of the night prostrate in adoration and prayer, begging forgiveness.

At daybreak, the priest was sent for. Many people and priests came to the house, and the Blessed Sacrament was processed to the church and encased in wax, while it was still bleeding, and put inside a tabernacle. Some years later, the tabernacle was opened and it was found that the wax had split into several pieces and instead the Host was contained in a pear-shaped glass pyx - another miracle. The pyx containing the Host has since been set into a specially crafted gold plated silver monstrance, which has 33 rays incorporated in the design. It is understood that St Francis Xavier visited the Miracle before embarking on his missionary journey to south India. The Host has bled fresh blood at different times. One such instance occurred in the 16th or 17th century when an unnamed bishop was overcome by curiosity, such that he broke open the top of the pyx to examine it, whereupon it bled, and the bishop was terrified; some versions say that he was the archbishop of Lisbon and that he died soon afterwards. Pilgrims have included royalty, and Lúcia of Fátima. In 1996-7 the shrine was authenticated by Cardinal Ratzinger – later Pope Benedict XVI – following analyses of some of the blood and the church consecrated as the **Church of The Most Holy Miracle Santarém** - though it is still often marked as Santo Estevão.

Following an earthquake in 1531, the church was reconstructed in the Renaissance style. Today, the monstrance is displayed on a tabernacle high up surrounded by an elaborate altarpiece. The custodian of the shrine will open doors and illuminate it for pilgrims in the church, however it can also be venerated close up. Behind the altarpiece are stairs to a corridor containing a small **museum** displaying votive offerings and portraits of some famous pilgrims. Then a ladder is climbed and there, we see the body and blood of Christ physically manifested, an experience unlikely to leave the pilgrim unmoved. The Host is irregular in shape with veins running through it to the bottom, where a quantity of blood is collected in a small chalice. Back in the nave, there are four paintings depicting the story, and a collection of tiles. The **house** of the couple was turned into a chapel in the 17th century, and is a short distance away (Travessa das Esteiras).

PILGRIMAGE INFORMATION

Directions: Along Rua Miguel Bombarda in a small square, Lago do Milagre. If you find yourself by the steps to the Cathedral, on the edge of the centre, then it is a walk of over 10 minutes in a straight line, along the pedestrianised streets without going downhill.

Open Mon – Sat 8.30AM – 5.30PM;
Sundays and Holidays by appointment only.

Feast day: Low Sunday. There is a procession through the streets.

To arrange a visit and for a private Mass write to: Escadinhas do Milagre 6, 2000-069 Santarém, Portugal; e-mail: *ssmilagre@gmail.com*;
Tel. +353 -243-329930;
Website: *http://www.santissimomilagresantarem.pt*

SIGHTS IN EASTERN SANTARÉM

Arguably the two finest sights in Santarém are close to the miracle church. A five minute walk along Bombarda, and a right turn down Primeiro Dezembro, brings us first to the **Misericórdia Church** from the 16th century with a later Baroque façade and then to the **Marvila church** (Praça Visconde Serra do Pilar). With its inter-woven carved motifs on the doorway it serves as one of the high points of Manueline church art. However it is the interior, clad from floor to ceiling with 17th century tiles, which has earned the church its fame as the 'tile cathedral'. Continue, turning right onto Julio Araújo and turning left at the end and we arrive at the beautiful Gothic **Nossa Senhora da Graça** church at **Largo Pedro Álvares Cabral** - there is a **statue** of the discoverer of Brazil (1467-1520) who is buried inside. First stand back to admire one of the finest rose windows you will ever see, and the flamboyant portal. Inside steps lead down to the three-nave church built in the late 14th century. Cabral is afforded national hero status, however, the elaborate tombs of the Menezes family, the church's founders and holders of the earldom of Ourém, are what stand out. Next to the church, going up Vila Belmonte, the **Casa do Brasil** belonged to the Cabral estate and today serves mostly as an exhibition space – with special reference to the Discoveries.

Now we make our way further up the street, turning right at the top and then onto Eng. Zeferino Sarmento. We come to two monuments opposite each other that serve as museums. The **Torre das Cabaças** served from the 15th century as a clock tower, and now has displays devoted to the measurement of time. The **church of São João de Alporão** (closed at time of writing) contains a collection of archaeology and medieval art. The church has some notable features of the Romanesque-Gothic transition. The walk down the long tree-lined street (Av. 5 de Outubro) that stretches out ahead, rewards the visitor with the views from the gardens of the **Portas do Sol**. We are on the site of the former castle and original walled town with two of its gates intact, royal palace, and much more before and since. Having admired the views from the walls, at the southern end of the gardens there is an **Interpretation Centre – Urbi Scallabis** which tells the story of the Roman settlement. At the northern end there are two buildings together. The **church of Santa Maria Alcáçova** was built in the 12th century over a Roman building as the headquarters in the town of the Knights Templar, and was the royal chapel. Its appearance today owes more to 18th century remodelling. Behind it is the **Passos-Canavarro Museum** in the house of a former politician, later the setting of a novel and then home to a collector of Japanese art. It is on the site of the royal palace built by Afonso Henriques following the conquest of Santarém. On the way out, off to the right is one of the gates, the **Porta de Santiago**. Here is the exit from the city of the **Caminho Portugués** – it is about 520Km to Santiago de Compostela with the next stages calling at Golegã and Tomar.

SIGHTS IN WESTERN SANTARÉM

Not far from the Miracle church is another attraction. The **Anselmo Braamcamp Freire Museum** (R. Braamcamp Freire) is in the former palace of the Barons of Almerim and contains a picture gallery and a library. Generally open when others are not! There are several pleasant squares and architectural features – including Manueline and Renaissance - to admire from one district to another. The **church of São Nicolau** (Largo Ramiro Nobre) was rebuilt in 1613 from a Gothic ruin in the Mannerist style. Inside is the fine 15th century tomb of João Afonso. From here turning up Rua Capelo e Ivens will take you past the **Tourist Office** and one or two *Pastelaria* that serve Santarém's famous *Celestes de Santa Clara* - almond cakes - and pampilhos – rolled cinnamon pastry topped with burnt sugar.

The end of the street brings you onto the Praça Sá da Bandeira, a square with several attractive features. On one side a wide set of steps leads up to the **Cathedral**. Dedicated to Our Lady of the Conception, it was originally the Jesuit church - after King João IV donated his palace site to the Society in 1647 - and that is most apparent once one enters. The grand façade is an example of the

Mannerist style that has nevertheless been modified. The interior's rich decoration is 18th century Baroque; the different coloured marble and twisted columns flanking the main altarpiece are but two of the themes favoured by the Jesuits who employed Italian architects. The ceiling of the nave – by a Portuguese painter - depicts the Assumption of Mary. The organ was made in England, later in 1835, and has recently been restored. The **Dicocesan Museum** was opened in 2014 and occupies part of the former Jesuit college. All rooms begin with representations of the Holy Trinity and there are many interesting items, notably a Baby Jesus curled on a rough-hewn Cross. Across the square is a Manueline **window** and in the far corner on the way out is the **church of Nossa Senhora da Piedade**. It was built by order of King Afonso VI to commemorate victory over Spain in the Battle of Ameixial (1663) during the Portuguese Restoration War – attributed to the intervention of the Virgin. Again, a combination of Mannerist façade and Baroque interior, it is the place for quiet prayer during the daytime.

Continue through, and come out on a major junction and gardens. Ahead left, the **municipal market** has attractive 1930s tile decoration. Turning right, make your way through the smaller República garden – passing to the left the **municipal offices** in the former palace of the Menezes - to the **Monastery of San Francisco**. Since deconsecrated and partly in ruins, this is nevertheless a fascinating space with many fine details preserved. Founded in 1242, the monastery takes in the Gothic, Manueline, Renaissance and Baroque. From the cloister, the church includes the remains of the high choir, initiated by King Ferdinand I in the 14th century to house his own tomb and that of his mother, Constanza. So, while the Franciscan friars had their base, so too did the nuns of

the Poor Clares. The **church of Santa Clara** can only be viewed from the outside at time of writing – walk on a little further and choose your vantage point. This is a solid Gothic structure with rose window, undergoing 17th century revisions. It was built in 1259 under the patronage of King Afonso III and continued under Queen Saint Isabel and her husband King Dinis.

One other church that should be mentioned is located beyond the larger Liberdad garden at Largo Cândido dos Reis. The **church of the Hospital of Jesus Christ** was built in the 17th and 18th centuries (remodelling) and is another in the Mannerist style. The internal features include a series of ceiling paintings and 17th century tiles. The former hospital has been turned into an education establishment and direct services in the fields of health and social care. Visits by appointment Tel. 243 30 52 60; e-mail: geral@scms.pt There are still more historic churches, chapels and other monuments and museums to visit as time allows. The city has a small range of accommodation in every category.

Another significant site 12Km west of Santarém (N365) is the Cistercian **Convent of Santa Maria de Almoster**. Having fallen into dilapidation in recent years, there has been a substantial restoration. However, at time of writing, you need to make prior arrangements for an internal visit; enquire at the Tourist Office. Arrive before reaching the centre of the town of Almoster. With its rose window at one end, this solid three-nave church bears strong resemblance to the church of Santa Clara. The convent was given papal approval in 1289 however it was only upon the intervention of Queen Saint Isabel in 1310 after the patron's death that the works were completed. The church includes restored altarpieces, sculptures, paintings, tiles and glass. The chapter house and cloister can also be seen.

RETURN JOURNEY

If you are returning to Fátima or just motoring around, there are some worthwhile stops amid beautiful countryside. **Almeirim** (N114) was a favourite hunting ground of the Avis dynasty. It is known for its wines, and in particular, for sopa da pedra a soup of meat, beans and vegetables with a stone at its base. A local legend has it that a beggar-priest tricked women of the town into gradually giving him all the ingredients by pretending to boil a stone. The stone was useless, of course, and it was a filling meal he was after. From here, the N118 takes us to **Alpiarça**. There are more manor houses, in particular the **Casa dos Patudos** which the collector José Relvas (1858-1929) – the man who declared the First Republic - left to the town. Inside is a magnificent array of furnishings, ceramics and porcelain. Paintings – there are hundreds - include Virgin with Child and St John (Tuscan School attributed to the School of Leonardo da Vinci), and Christ in the Tomb (Spanish school, Alonso David, 19th century). There is an extensive archive including photographs. If the architecture has some familiar touches, that is because Raul Lino was the architect – much in demand at Sintra. Entrance €2.50; Closed Mondays.

In Golegã, the mother **church** has a fine Manueline portal. **Casa-Estúdio Carlos Relvas** (Largo Dom Manuel I) is a photographic collection of the father of José Relvas in a stunning house. In the first half of November, **Feira Nacional do Cavalo** (National Horse Fair) takes place. Six Km further northeast (IC3 from Golegã) **Quinta da Cardiga** is a fine palace, once belonging to the Order of Christ and retaining part of their fortifications. It was remodelled in the 16th century. Available to someone with deep pockets at time of writing.

Torres Novas, with its historic **bridge** and **water wheel**, is situated on the Almonda river. Its turbulent history has seen Roman occupation, several conflicts between Moors and Christians, the Spanish and the French, and its near-abandonment in the 1830s following support for the absolutist Miguel during the struggle for succession. The **castle** has a wall with 11 towers and gardens. The **Museu Municipal Carlos Reis** (Rua do Salvador) has several Roman artefacts such as from nearby Villa Cardilio, together with sacred art and the paintings of Reis. Of the several churches: **Misericórdia** (Praça 5 Outubro) has a Renaissance portico; **Santiago** (Adro de Santiago) has a figure of Christ Crucified on its altarpiece and references to St James, although the Camino no longer passes through; **Salvador** (Largo do Salvador) has rich gold and tile decoration; **São Pedro** (Largo de S. Pedro) dates from the 14th century with Gothic, Baroque and Rococo elements.

Part 10
VISIT TO NAZARÉ

Today's excursion involves a 45-minute drive from Fátima to the coast to visit an historic fishing town with a wide sandy beach, which houses two important shrines to one legend. In effect, there are two towns. **Sítio** is a headland the top of which provides a sheer 300 metre drop to the beach. It houses a wide square with bandstand, which fills with sizzling fish stalls during the festivals and contains the church and chapel to the shrine, together with several restaurants leading off. A **funicular** (€1.20 single) connects to the beach and **promenade**, where there are still remnants of Nazaré's fishing past. Coloured **boats** with a high prow to deflect the surf used to be pulled out of the water by oxen, later by tractor. The fish wives still dry and sell the mackerel on racks, while renting out beach tents. Traditionally they wore seven petticoats under a full skirt, caps and earrings, and today still look distinctive. The fishermen wore stocking caps, bright shirts and ¾ length trousers. They claim to be descended from the Phoenicians, and you can detect possible hints in their long thin noses and grey eyes – some

of the boats also sport a painted eye. Most of the fishing has transferred to a modern harbour at the south end of the promenade. In the summer the beach and hotels are packed with tourists. Along with Peniche, Nazaré ranks among the world's premier surfing destinations, hosting the leading tour competitions, the best waves formed by an enormous underwater canyon.

It is a good idea to explore Sítio first especially if you have a car, and take the funicular down to the beach and back up again.

PILGRIM VISITS

On the edge of the square by the cliff edge, the **Memória Chapel** commemorates two connected stories 468 years apart. In 714 a monk who was accompanied by Roderic, the Visigothic king, brought a Black Madonna to the site from a monastery near Mérida where they fled the Moors, and decided to become a hermit, living in a grotto. When he died he was buried in the grotto with the statue on an altar. Legend has it that one foggy morning in 1182,

nobleman Dom Fuas Roupinho of Porto de Mós was hunting a stag who was really the devil in disguise. It disappeared over the cliff edge, while the man and his horse plunged over in pursuit. At that point the Virgin Mary appeared and pulled them back to safety. The Templar knight had the chapel built above the grotto; it is said he had known of the statue and venerated it whenever he was in the area. Of course, that is how the miracle was attributed, and a pilgrimage quickly grew up. People peer over the precipice to see if they can make out a mark in the rock said to have been made by the horse's hoof.

The chapel is on two levels, with the lower floor displaying tiled allegories of the legend on its vaulted ceiling. Access to the cave is not permitted; however, a replica of the image is displayed on a niche.

The **statue** of the Virgin and Child was, according to a document found in the grotto, brought to Mérida from Nazareth – hence the name of the town – where it is believed it was sculpted by St Joseph and painted by St Luke. It is certainly a few centuries old, though probably not as old as that. A separate **Church of Our Lady of Nazaré** was built to house it under the orders of King Ferdinand I in

1377 in order to cope with the pilgrims, many of whom were generous, and as a result of royal patronage. The Sanctuary was enlarged several times from the 16th to the 19th century. Inside, the statue is placed high on an elaborate Baroque altarpiece with gilded ceiling above. There is a small charge (€1) to visit the statue. To do so is a journey in itself, by entering a tiled corridor to one side of the altar, and after several turns, arriving in a chapel with a metal staircase. At the top of the stairs, flanked by more tiles and two large paintings, enter a doorway to turn and finally stand in front of the clothed and crowned statue. Back in the single nave church, the tiles in the transept by a Dutch artist are particularly fine. The

festival - including the procession of the Virgin - takes place on September 8th with various events beginning at the end of August and lasting for two weeks. Venerations of the Virgin of Nazaré are common throughout the region, some with their own local festivals.

The **Dr Joaquim Manso Museum** tells the story of the people and customs of Nazaré; Open Tues. – Fri.; Admission €2; Rua Dom Fuas Roupinho that leads off the square. At the end of the promontory is the **São Miguel Arcanjo Fort**. Built in the 16th century, it was attacked by Napoleon's troops in 1808 and the town sacked. It makes another great viewpoint.

Seven Km south, close to the sea, the **Chapel of São Gião** is one of the few Visigothic churches that survive in Portugal. From there it is a similar distance further to **São Martinho do Porto**, a very picturesque and altogether quieter piece of the coastline.

Part 11
VISIT TO ÓBIDOS AND CALDAS DE RAINHA

This excursion involves nearly an hour's driving time each way, but is worth it to see two towns whose histories are centuries apart, and whose attractions are similarly contrasting. Those on a driving tour of the country should certainly consider staying overnight in the charming walled town of Óbidos which has a range of historic accommodation, while the Spa town of Caldas de Rainha has a more limited range of hotels including one built on the site of the former grand hotel. For the golfer, a better option might be to stay at the accommodation associated with the three top class courses in the area.

CALDAS DE RAINHA

As the name implies, this town owes its existence to its curative spa with royal patronage. In 1484 Queen Leonor, wife of King João II, was travelling from Óbidos to Batalha when she saw - and smelt – some poor peasants bathing in the hot sulphurous water. She stopped and enquired what they were doing, and they explained that the water relieved a number of ailments. One version of the story has it that the Queen immediately immersed, as she too was suffering from a complaint. She resolved to create better conditions for the people and ordered a hospital to be built. Over the centuries a line of monarchs visited the spa and a new wing was built in the 19th century; today it still treats rheumatism, arthritis, and sinusitis. There was an aborted attempt at the Captains' Coup on March 16th 1974. It seemed only the 30 officers and 300 men of the Caldas De Rainha barracks were ready so they turned back from Lisbon and were placed under arrest, until the actual 'Red Carnation' Revolution a month later. The area is noted for its local clay and so pottery has been a feature for centuries. Caldas de Rainha is home to the world famous Bordalo Pinheiro ceramics factory. Today, the historic part of the town, its Art Nouveau houses with tiled fronts and wrought iron balconies, is somewhat faded while there are modern districts and facilities, but it does not lack for atmosphere and beauty.

The best place to start is the oblong Praça da República, where Portugal's only **daily farmers' market** is held. In the northeast corner of the square is the

chapel of São Sebastião which was originally 16th century Mannerist and was rebuilt by João V in the Baroque style. From here take any of the passageways off right and soon you will come to the **Thermal Hospital Rainha D. Leonor**. Attached at one end of it is the **church of Nossa Señora do Pópulo** (Our Lady of the People). Originally it was the royal chapel of the hospital but was soon made the mother church of the town. Its interior features a triptych of the Passion over a 16th century triumphal arch, which is flanked by two 18th century carved side altars. They are mounted on plinths covered with Mozarabic tiles. The former royal palace now houses a **medical museum** dedicated to the spa's history.

Beyond the hospital, take the road alongside the park until you reach an institution of world ceramics. **Rafael Bordalo Pinheiro** (1846-1905) was not only a potter, but also a celebrated cartoonist. The two skills combined in his

outlandish designs: salad bowls shaped as cabbage leaves; frogs on water lilies; a peasant woman; a civil guard. The outlet shop neighbours a **museum** (by appointment or ask in the shop) with original pieces. A little further south are three **art museums** that show the works of two sculptors and a painter. Cross over to walk back to the centre through the **Parque Dom Carlos I**. It is attractively laid out with mature trees and flower beds, and a boating lake. It also contains another of the town's art museums, **Museu José Malhoa** which shows contemporary works and more Bordalo Pinheiro pottery. Finally, the **Ceramics Museum** is located in the

southeast of the town at Rua Doutor Ilídio Amado.

Foz do Arelho is a small resort eight Km west of Caldas de Rainha. It has access both to the sea two Km away and the **Óbidos Lagoon**. The lagoon is a reminder that the sea used to come in much further than today.

ÓBIDOS

With such a commanding hilltop position, it is no surprise that both 4th century BC remains of a Celtic Castro that would have looked down on water, and Roman fortifications dating from 1st century AD, have been found in Óbidos. After brief Visigothic occupation, the Moors took up residence that would last nearly half a millennium. Óbidos was only captured in 1148, some nine years after Afonso Henriques had become king. Successive kings improved the fortifications though you can still see the Moorish battlements today. In 1195 it is believed King Sancho I granted the town its first charter. King Afonso II bestowed Óbidos to his wife Queen Urraca, and when King Dinis married Isabel there in 1282 and made it part of her dowry, it became the property of successive queens of Portugal. For this reason Óbidos is known as the *Casa das Reinhas* – House of the Queens. But perhaps its most famous daughter is Josefa de Ayala y Cabrera (1630-84) a painter of religious scenes who became known as **Josefa d'Óbidos**; several examples of her work can be seen. Just south, **Roliça** was the setting in 1808 for the first battle fought by British forces with their Portuguese allies – commanded by Sir Arthur Wellesley, later Duke of Wellington – in the Peninsular War. Prior to the battle, the British vanguard met the French rearguard at Óbidos. Nowadays this gem, with its whitewashed houses adorned with bougainvillea and honeysuckle, has certainly been discovered, and only by staying overnight will you get the sense of having the place to yourself. That said, not everyone braves the walk around the walls, as

there are many uneven patches and care is needed. It is the ideal way to observe the town's architecture and overall layout. Down at ground level, there are many charms, with cultural attractions too.

There are several gateways. The one on the east side of the town close to the main square and castle is dedicated to **Our Lady of Grace**, an open-air

chapel housing the statue in a glass case with tiled background. Another gate generally considered to be the main one – Porta da Villa – is dedicated to **Our Lady of Piety – or Sorrows** and has tiles depicting the Passion and a painted ceiling, all added in the 18ᵗʰ century. **The Castle and Royal Palace** which is now the Pousada are at the north end. The palace was added in the reign of King Manuel I with typical windows, but was still in ruins from the 1755 earthquake when the state chain came to restore it in the 20th century – the first of its hotels in an historic building.

Rua Direita is the main street and acts as an artery from one end of the walled town – Porta da Villa - to the other, the castle. Running parallel is the Rua Josefa d'Óbidos. Alternatively, if you are walking the walls, there are steps down at different points. Prior to entering the Porta da Villa just ahead of where the tour buses stop, is the **church of São João Baptista.** Possibly built on the site of a

Visigothic church, it was founded by Queen Saint Isabel in 1309 close to the leprosarium she endowed and was dedicated to St Vincent. Restored, it now houses the Parish Museum; closed Mondays. Passing through the gate we come to a square with two

religious monuments. The **Church of São Pedro** was originally Gothic and rebuilt after the earthquake. One of the survivors is the gilded altarpiece from the late 17th century. Josefa d' Óbidos is buried here. The **chapel of São Martinho** dates from 1331 and was originally the family chapel of the Lords of Pó.

The next square – Santa Maria - is the main one. The stone **Pillory** is decorated with a carved fishing net in honour of Queen Leonor's son Afonso who was recovered by fishermen after his fatal accident in 1491. The **church of Santa Maria** is the mother church of the town. Again, it may have been a Visigothic church, and was the site of a mosque during Moorish occupation. Like São Pedro, it once had a college of canons. It is where in 1441 the King Afonso V aged 10 and Isabel aged eight were married – Portugal was under a regency as clearly Afonso was far too young to rule! The fine Renaissance portal has an image of Our Lady of the Assumption in a niche. There is much to admire, including paintings on the main altarpiece by João da Costa c.1620 while the ones of St Catherine on a side altarpiece are by Josefa d'Óbidos. There are more of her works, together with those of other painters such as André Reinoso, in the **Municipal Museum** in a former manor house in the square; closed Mondays. There are various other **galleries** around, mostly dedicated to contemporary art. Just off the square behind the Museum, is the **church of the Misericórdia**. It was built by Queen Leonor in 1498 and originally served the purpose of an alms house and hospital. It has a blue porcelain statue of the Virgin in its porch while the interior is covered in tiles from the 17th century.

By the side of the castle is the **church of Santiago**. Built by King Sancho I in 1186, it was used by the royal family; originally its west door went straight into the castle. Completely rebuilt after the earthquake, the altarpiece dedicated to St James is now in the Municipal Museum. The sixteenth century **Aqueduct** was built by Queen Catherine, wife of João III to transport water to the town and is intact at three Km in length.

There are more churches and chapels outside the walls including: **Nossa**

Senhora de Monserrate with tiled façade; **Nossa Senhora de Carmo** which has its origins in a Roman temple dedicated to Jupiter. Also the **Sanctuary of Senhor Jesus da Pedra** (Our Lord Jesus of the Stone) – this unusual Baroque church sits on the Caldas de Rainha road looking up at the town and was built by King João V after he invoked the patron to escape from an accident.

Óbidos has many **festivals**, some traditional to the town and other more recent innovations. Holy Week has several processions – including the Passion of Christ on Palm Sunday - and services in all the main churches. Check the websites www.cm-obidos.pt and www.obidos.pt for the up-to-date programme. Of the other religious festivals, the main ones are: Romaria de Santo Antão, January 17th; Festa de Santa Cruz with fair of traditional produce on May 3rd; Festa de Santa Iria with fair, October 20th. The town is nowadays famous for its **Medieval Fair** with everything from jousting and jesters to hearty meals; reduced entrance fee if you go in medieval dress; mid July to early August. Óbidos is known for its **chocolate** production and a festival offers more opportunities than usual to celebrate; most of April. Finally, we cannot leave Óbidos without sampling its most famous product, **Ginja**. A morello cherry liqueur from an old recipe, expertly blended so that it combines the sweet and the sour, some shops offer the opportunity to drink a sample out of a chocolate cup which you then eat.

PENICHE

A fishing and seaside town 24Km west of Óbidos, Peniche lies on a peninsular that was once an island. Several hotels have access onto the long beaches on one side with cliffs on the other. The way down to the **port** is lined with fish restaurants, and has the **old town** behind it. The large **castle** was built in the 16th century, and later used as a prison for some of the most prominent opponents of the Estado Novo; there is a **lighthouse**. There are several historic churches:- one - the **Misericórdia** - has many paintings including by Josefa d'Óbidos. The **Sanctuary of Remédios** has its festival in October. The **Festa do Nossa Senhora da Boa Viagem** features land and sea processions in August. Peniche is also traditionally well-known for its lace making. The **Berlengas islands**, 10Km offshore, are a nature reserve that can be reached by boat trip. *www.cm-peniche.pt*

Part 12
VISIT TO COIMBRA

Another frequently-made visit for Fátima pilgrims is to the convent where Lúcia spent much of her long life. The journey by bus or car is of one hour from Fátima and two hours from Lisbon, from where train journeys vary according to which service is taken – there is a faster train that goes on to Porto. Coimbra is mid-way between Lisbon and Porto. It is best known for its ancient university and has a lot of history.

Occupying both riverside and high hilltop locations, Coimbra was developed by the Romans as the new town of Aeminium after their original city to the south - **Conimbriga** which can be visited today – became less advantageous to transport routes by land and water. The frontage of the river Mondego was further developed as a port after the reconquest of this part of Portugal by King Ferdinand I of León and Castile in 1064 – more than 80 years before the Kingdom of Portugal was declared. The first two Portuguese kings are buried here, and at one time Coimbra served as the capital. Queen Saint Isabel, the city's patroness, spent her last years from 1325 in the original convent of Santa Clara as a Poor Clare, having given away her wealth. King João I was crowned here in 1385. The University was founded in 1290 and like its near contemporaries Cambridge and Oxford in England, has served for centuries as the premier seat of learning in the country. Even today, many of the students can be seen in their black capes, bearing a different coloured ribbon according to which faculty they are studying – until the end of the academic year when they ceremonially burn the ribbons. The students gave birth to one of the styles of *Fado* music, which has more intellectual lyrics, but to many visitors will sound no less melancholy. The architecture of the **Coimbra school** is of the Renaissance style and began when King Manuel I brought the French sculptors Jean de Rouen and Nicolas Chanterene to Portugal in 1518. Portugal's most famous poet Luis de Camões is strongly associated with Coimbra, as is mathematician Pedro Nunes. Today, the city's population of 105,000 is part of a wider municipality and then district. As with other academic centres, there is an emphasis on high technology and medical research.

In terms of orientation for the visitor, the city divides into three districts: The *Alta* (Upper Town) for the fit can be climbed through narrow stepped streets and contains the University, cathedrals and many other monuments; the *Baixa* (Lower Town) leads to the river and the rail station *(Coimbra-A)* and has many good, cheap restaurants and typical Portuguese architecture; the Santa Clara is across the bridge and has the old and new convents of Clares. Everything can be covered in one full day, though you will need longer if you are to include the museums in depth and more of the churches. Good grippy shoes are essential.

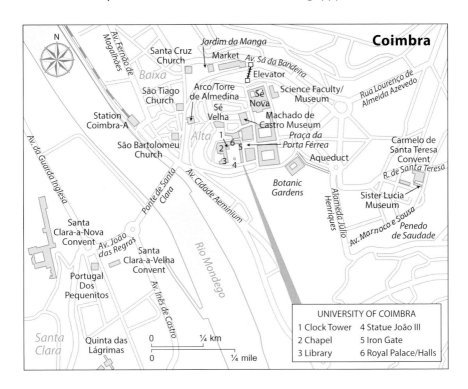

THE CARMELO DE SANTA TERESA

The convent of Discalced Carmelites is located 15 or so minutes' walk beyond the sights of the *Alta*. If you have visited the University, keep walking through a large square and head down, then right under the **Aqueduct** and through the pleasant **Botanic Gardens**; leave the gardens at the end up steps, turn left to the Avenue; turn right and then cross left onto Av. Marnoco e Sousa, following it up and round until you reach the entrance to the Sister Lúcia Museum at the side of the convent. There is car parking alongside – especially if you arrive at lunchtime prior to the museum's reopening. Alongside Marnoco e Sousa are pleasant **hillside gardens** – *Penedo da Saudade* - with memorials to leading academics.

Sister Lúcia came from the Dorothean Sisters at Tui in Spain, entering the convent in Coimbra in March 1948, and made her profession on May 31st 1949 as Sister Maria Lúcia of Jesus and the Immaculate Heart. She remained there until her death on February 13th 2005 having been visited several times by the Virgin Mary. In addition to all of the prayer and sacrifice as a nun, Lúcia was kept busy answering the stream of correspondence and reading prayer requests that came in from around the world, including requests for her intercession for the curing of the sick. She returned to Fátima on rare occasions.

Outside the front entrance, a large **statue** was erected in 2013. There are always fresh flowers in the surrounding bed. Inside the entrance, one can usually enter the convent **chapel**. Here one can see where Lúcia prayed: the choir through the grille, and the gilded dark wood altarpieces. The recently opened museum is called the *Memorial Irmã Lúcia*. Inside are some of Lúcia's few possessions: rosaries, habit, spectacles and her electric typewriter. There are some objects used by her at the time of the apparitions. There is a replica of her cell, and also a small theatre that shows a video of her life. As this is a working convent, of 18 sisters, it is not always possible to see other parts, such as the garden and the images of the Immaculate Heart of Mary. http://coimbra.carmelitas.pt

THE LOWER TOWN

We start by the **Municipal Market** where there is reasonably priced car parking. Behind the market is an **elevator** – not always in service – that is one way to reach the Upper Town. The main attraction in this part of the *Baixa* is the **Church of Santa Cruz**. Its entrance is in the square, Praça 8 de Maio, the start of a long wide pedestrianised street that leads to the river and the Santa Clara district. Part of an Augustinian monastery, the church was originally Romanesque, but the Manueline façade and Baroque porch are parts in a series of modifications. Some of the busts of the portal are from the Coimbra school, as is the magnificent pulpit and the tombs of Kings Afonso Henriques and Sancho I - making this one of Portugal's national pantheons. The high choir is worth seeking out, as is the cloister -

Tomb of King Afonso Henriques   *Arco de Almedina*

part of which leads into the **Jardim da Manga** with its lemon yellow fountain, again in Renaissance style.

At the **Arco e Torre de Almedina** - a remnant of the 11th century walls and Moorish occupation - you can pass through the gateway to take the picturesque and tiring route to the sights of the *Alta*. There is also a **museum** in the tower. Continuing in the Lower Town, however, you can make a small detour right into the Praça do Comércio for two churches. At the top of the square, the **Church of Santiago** (*São Tiago*) is a Romanesque church of the late 12th century, although some say that it was founded originally by Ferdinand I after he captured the city. At the opposite end of the square, in R. Dos Esteiros, the **Church of São Bartolomeu** (St Bartholomew) does date back to the 10th century although it owes its present appearance to 18th century remodelling. The large panel in the altarpiece depicts the martyrdom of the church's patron.

Walking further down leads us to Largo do Portagem and the wide boulevard and **riverside gardens** - *Parque Manuel Braga* - alongside the river. You can walk straight across the **Ponte de Santa Clara** to the convents. However, turning right and then right again by the rail station onto Largo das Ameias can lead us to discover another part of the *Baixa* - the narrow streets that can lead us back to the start. North of the Market, Rua da Sofia has more churches and remnants of the ancient University.

THE UPPER TOWN

From the Almedina route, the first monument you arrive at is the **Old Cathedral** *(Sé Velha)*. A sturdy Romanesque-Gothic structure with battlements and slit lower windows, dating from the 12th century, the church was also used as a defensive bastion. On the left side there is a 16th century portal by Jean de Rouen. The main altarpiece is in flamboyant late Gothic and by Flemish artists, while the chapels to either side are from the Coimbra school. The cloister was built in the early Gothic style and is the oldest surviving in Portugal. Many pilgrims will additionally make their trip to Portugal a pilgrimage to **St Anthony of Padua**, visiting his birthplace in Lisbon. Here is where he was ordained as a priest and discovered the Franciscan order. The square is the traditional centre of student nightlife, with *Fado* still performed.

Moving on, keeping as straight as possible,

University: Porta Férrea

94

the **Museu Nacional de Machado de Castro** entrance (Largo Dr. José Rodrigues) is diagonally opposite the **New Cathedral** *(Sé Nova)*. Internationally recognised, the museum is built over the Roman forum, the remains of which can be toured. The extensive collection is especially strong on religious art, including a thorough understanding of the styles that contributed to the Coimbra school. The Cathedral was consecrated as such in 1772. It was begun by the Jesuits as their headquarters in the city, until their suppression by the Marquês de Pombal in 1759. The upper façade was finished in Baroque whereas the lower part is sober Mannerist. There are several Baroque altarpieces and the reliquaries in the transept are said to include St Luke and St Francis Xavier. To the right of the Cathedral is the Science faculty favoured by Pombal and behind it is the **Science Museum** – occupying the first Jesuit college in the world.

THE UNIVERSITY

Since 2013 the University facilities have been included on the UNESCO World Heritage list. The undoubted highlight is the quadrangle housing the former royal palace which was donated to the University by King João III in the 16th century, and the buildings that were added. The conquerors effectively took over the headquarters of the Moorish fortress as their own, before it developed into a palace.

Walk back past the Machado de Castro Museum down Rua de Sao João, turning right onto Praça da Porta Férrea. The square is named after the **'iron gate'** to the University quadrangle. The stone façades at the entrance and exit were built in the 17th century; the statues include King João and King Dinis, the figure above is Knowledge – the symbol of the University - while the female figures represent the three faculties at the time, Law and Medicine on the outside, Theology and Canon Law on the inside. Towards the end, left, is a **statue** of King João III and a **terrace** with views of the city. In front on the opposite side are the famous Library and the Chapel. Visitors to the **Library** are admitted in small groups every 20 minutes and photography is not allowed. A strong contender for the world's most stunning college library, it was a gift from King João V in the early 18th century. It shouts empire, yet within a century of it being built, Brazil had won its full independence. The 60,000 16th – 18th century books are protected from insects by a colony of bats. Downstairs is the **book deposit**, and below that, the intriguing **Academic Prison** where seditious students were locked up – until the 1830s the University had its own legal code and guards. A door and stairs lead back to the quadrangle. The **Chapel of São Miguel** is essentially Manueline in style and remained a royal chapel after being gifted to the University. It has a late 17th century painted ceiling. On the left, the altar is dedicated to Our Lady of Light, patroness of students.

At the other end in the corner is the 18th century **clock tower** with bells, one of which – the 'goat' - calls students to class. The University main halls and former Royal Palace are up the **Via Latina** - the exterior staircase and colonnade. The **Sala dos Capelos** - also known as the Great Hall of Acts - is where important academic ceremonies take place and you will normally look down into this room from a gallery. It was originally the throne room in which in 1385 João I was proclaimed as King of Portugal and has large portraits of the kings on its walls. Also to be seen is the **Armoury** besides the **Examination Room** with portraits of past rectors. At time of writing, back at ground level there was an exhibition of royal portraits in a **gallery**.

Ticket prices depend upon how much you wish to see:
from €5 up to €12 for self-guided
and €12.50 - €20 for guided;
up to €15 with radio guides.
http://visit.uc.pt/en

SANTA CLARA

Cross the bridge – the Caminho Portugués enters Coimbra in the opposite direction (370Km approx. to Santiago de Compostela) – and head towards the ruins on the left. The ruined Gothic Convent of Santa Clara-a-Velha was occupied until 1677, when it was abandoned for the new convent. The building was prone to flooding from the river, and sufficient knowledge to defend it

from the waters did not exist at the time. It was increasingly buried in mud, and was excavated from 1995. It is now protected by flood barriers, and there is an interpretation centre allowing access and displaying some of the finds. Santa Clara-a-Nova is further up the hill. Closed at time of writing, it is due to reopen in 2017 following extensive renovation. Queen Saint Isabel's tomb was removed here, and is incorporated in the magnificent main altarpiece. There is also a statue and a series of paintings dedicated to her life, and the lives of St Francis and St Clare.

On the way to the new convent, **Portugal dos Pequenitos** is not only for children; there are scale models of famous Portuguese monuments and styles of houses. **Quinta das Lágrimas** is nowadays a luxury hotel and is an 18th century rebuild. It was much earlier that Pedro I installed here his mistress Inés de Castro (see story p.62) the subject of a poem by Camões. The garden has a spring that is said to have emerged from the ground where she was murdered.

Part 13
LISBON

Portugal's capital is famous for being built on seven hills, leading down to the wide and sheltered river Tagus (*Tejo*). Archaeology reveals human remains from as far back as 7000BC and certainly by 3000BC there was a settled population. The Celts / Indo Europeans and the more Germanic Lusitani who followed were able to mine gold, tin and copper. This attracted those maritime traders, the Phoenicians, with evidence of a trading post on the site of the Cathedral leading down to the river. The Carthaginians certainly had a presence on the east of the Iberian peninsular, until they were defeated by the Romans in the Punic wars. In 137BC the Republic went west and took the settlement by that time known as *Olissipo*: Was this a legacy of the Phoenicians or was Odysseus' discovery more than a myth? Either way, it was renamed *Felicitas Julia* after Julius Caesar and its population – whoever they were – given Roman citizenship. Walls defended it from Lusitanian raids, and during the long reign of Augustus temples, a necropolis, forum, amphitheatre and baths were built. Christianity began to take root here, with several martyrs. The Barbaric Suebi were followed by the Visigoths who re-established Lisbon as a significant religious centre. However in 714 Moorish Berbers and Arabs conquered the city. They remained for 400 years, naming it *Aschbouna* and turned it into a centre of learning, trade and prosperity. Jews and Mozarabic Christians were tolerated and played important roles in the city's life. The Alfama district is a survivor from that time. After a raid in 1108 by Norwegian crusaders under Sigurd I on their way to the Holy Land, the city was finally conquered in 1147 by Afonso Henriques, who built the Baixa district.

From then on, the history of Lisbon was in effect the history of Portugal, of all its colourful triumphs and tragedies. The Age of Discoveries brought traders from Germany, France, Flanders and Italy, and the British who through their Lisbon Factory established the longest lasting foreign community that survives to this day. The novelist **Henry Fielding** died in Lisbon, with a monument to him at the British cemetery at **St George's Church**, Estrela. They were all but wiped out along with 40,000 of the population and 20,000 buildings in the great **earthquake** of 1755 and its aftermath. With one of the largest seaports in Europe, Lisbon today is a cosmopolitan city, which despite the lurches of successive economic crises, has managed to shake off much of the poverty that characterised it in the past - although the shanty towns occupying some of the hills have not exactly disappeared. The city itself has a population of 550,000 while the much wider Lisbon Region extends south of the Tagus to Setúbal.

VISITING

With well in excess of 1.5 million tourists annually, Lisbon is one of the most visited cities in Europe, and they come from every part of the world. There is a lot to see, with the hilly nature of the city and Portuguese paving providing a test of stamina – good walking shoes or trainers are a must. Broadly speaking there are four areas of the city for the visitor. The central districts of Alfama, Baixa – the rebuilt area laid out by the Marquês de Pombal as a grid following the earthquake - Bairro Alto and Chiado are next to eachother and contain more than half the main sights. To the north of these, the areas laid out in the 19th century branching out from the big Marquês de Pombal roundabout/square include the Edward VII Park, the Botanic Garden and the gardens and Basilica of Estrela. Thirdly, the western district of Belém is perhaps the most visited, as it contains the iconic Discoveries monument, Tower and the Jerónimos Monastery. The long stretch of river from there to the Tiles Museum, often known as the *Ribeira*, takes in the suspension bridge and the Praça do Comércio - which can also be reached on foot from the central districts. It seems everywhere there are churches.

As you would expect, tour groups are well catered for and a selection of sights will be included in an itinerary. This will always include Belém, and for **pilgrim travellers**, there will often be a visit and perhaps Mass at the church and shrine to St Anthony of Padua which is by Lisbon's Cathedral in the Alfama. For independent travellers, it is perfectly possible to **drive in Lisbon** contrary to the many dire warnings. Marquês de Pombal, though, can be hectic, and Belém near impossible to park. One can often park opposite the Tiles Museum. Always try to include a crossing of the Tagus on the suspension bridge. The central districts get congested at night with people coming to eat.

Lisbon's historic yellow **Trams** are a must. The No. 28 Tram will connect you with the sights in the Alfama's narrow steep streets and squares, and beyond. The public transport system is good and includes a **Metro** with four lines – blue,

yellow, green and red – and a **bus and rail network**. You can use the latter or the **express buses** to make day trips to Sintra, Santarém, and Coimbra while staying in Lisbon. The modern train terminal is Oriente; however it is easy to get to many of the places you want starting at Rossio station in the centre. The main bus company operating services to the rest of Portugal is Rede Expressos www.rede-expressos.pt Always use this option when going to Fátima as it does not have a rail station. The bus station is at Sete Rios - blue Metro line stop Jardim Zoológico, two minutes' walk. Lisbon Airport is at Portela in the northeast of the city. On arrival, the

Aerobus service is especially useful if you have a reservation at one of the central hotels, or you can take the red Metro line (for most central districts change to green at Alameda and take line heading *Sul*). Many cheaper car rental firms are off airport – you are met on arrival, but have to find the depot on your return! The **Lisboa Card** (from €18.50) is issued by the Tourist Offices and provides entry to many of the museums and travel on public transport. With museum concessions, free Sundays, combined tickets and cheap multi-use transport tickets, do weigh up your options. On Mondays many attractions are closed.

BELÉM

Before exploring the other districts we head west, away from the centre, for the waterside district – once a separate village - from which many of the great explorers set sail on their Voyages of Discovery. They included Vasco da Gama in 1497 on his discovery of India and two years later, Pedro Álvares Cabral on his discovery of Brazil. Later, it was where the royal family had their palaces.

In 1496 King Manuel I sought permission from the Pope to construct a monastery on the site of a small church belonging to the Order of Christ, and construction began around 1502, with the money coming from a tax on the spice trade. The King wanted a monastery dedicated to the Discoveries and the memory of the *Infante Henriques* – Prince Henry the Navigator. A community of Hieronymite monks – of the Order of St Jerome who follow the Rule of St Augustine - would offer spiritual assistance to seafarers and pray for the King. The façade of **Jerónimos Monastery** with its incredibly ornate south doorway is in the distinctly Portuguese late Gothic style known as Manueline, with the master architect Diogo de Boitaca being succeeded by the Spaniard Juan de Castillo, who introduced Plateresque elements. There is also work by the French sculptors Nicolas Chanterene – who did the west door, now inside - and Jean de Rouen, both of the Coimbra school founded by Manuel. When Manuel died in 1521 construction was suspended, resuming in 1550 with the Renaissance architect Diogo de Torralva, who completed the main chapel, choir and monks' quarters in

Monument to the Discoveries

Tower of Belem

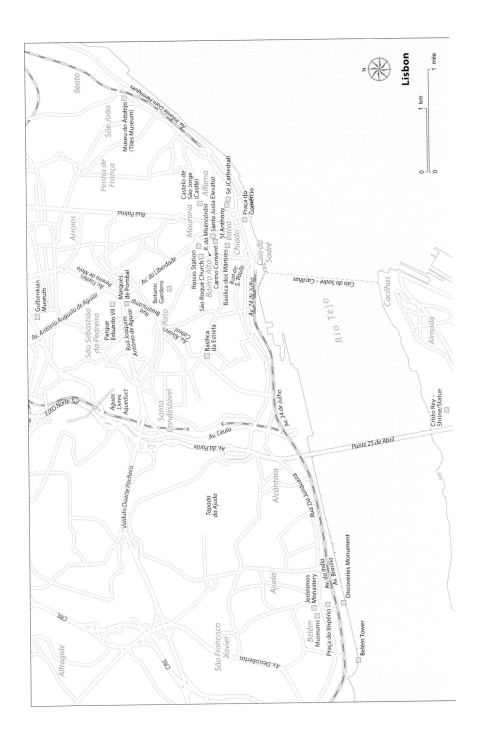

Lisbon

N

0   1 km
0   1 mile

Beato

São João

Museu do Azulejo
(Tiles Museum)

Av. Infante Dom Henriques

Penha de
França

Arroios

Rua Palma

Mouraria

Alfama

Castelo de
São Jorge
(Castle)

Sé (Cathedral)

St Anthony
Santa Justa Elevator

Praça do
Comércio

Gulbenkian
Museum

Av. Fontes
Pereira de Melo

Marquês
de Pombal

Av. da Liberdade

Botanic
Gardens

Rossio Station

São Roque Church

R. da Misericórdia

Carmo Convent

Basílica dos Mártires

Bairro Alto

Chiado

Baixa

Rua de
S. Paulo

Cais do
Sodré

Av. 24 de Julho

Cais do Sodré – Cacilhas

Cacilhas

Almada

Av. António Augusto de Aguiar

São Sebastião
da Pedreira

Parque
Eduardo VII

Rua Joaquim
António de Aguiar

Rato

Av. Álvares
Cabral

Rua
Braamcamp

Basílica
da Estrela

Rio Tejo

EIXO Norte-Sul

Águas
Livres
Aqueduct

Santo
Condestável

Av. Ceuta

Av. da Ponte

Av. 24 de Julho

Ponte 25 de Abril

Cristo Rey –
Shrine/Statue

Viaduto Duarte Pacheco

Tapada
da Ajuda

Alcântara

Rua Da Junqueira

Ajuda

Jerónimos
Monastery

Av. da Índia

Av. Brasília

Discoveries Monument

CRIL

Alfragide

São Francisco
Xavier

Belém

Museums

Praça do Império

Av. Descobertas

Belém Tower

105

THE BAIXA

The grid of the rebuilt town is mostly known for its shops, cafes and pastry shops, apart from its architecture. Many of the 18th century buildings have acquired Art Nouveau fronts and interiors. We are going to concentrate on three areas - what sights lie at either end and to one side.

Opening onto the waterside is the most dramatic of city squares, the **Praça do Comércio**. It is approached via R. Augusta through a **triumphal arch**, with a large **statue** of King José I on horseback. Here is the site of the Ribeira Palace which was never rebuilt following the earthquake. Next to the **west tower**, the new **Lisbon Story Centre** tells in an innovative way of this city's momentous history. At the start of the grid of streets, there is a fascinating subterranean Roman find: the **Núcleao Archaeológico da Rua dos Correiros** below the BCP Bank. Up the next street Rua da Prata, and right onto

The Rua Augusta arch leads onto Praça do Comércio

Rua da Vitória, the **Church of São Nicolau** is noted for its ceilings, painted by Pedro Alexandrino de Carvalho and representing Faith, Hope and Charity.

At the north end of the Baixa, the grid system opens out onto a series of connected squares. To the left is **Praça Dom Pedro IV**, or **Rossio Square**. There are two **fountains** and a **statue** of the King on a tall pedestal, while the Neoclassical **Teatro Nacional Dona Maria II** is on the north side. Off to the right of this, the façade of the **Church of São Domingos** dominates its own square. Originally part of a monastery, it was the scene in 1506 of the killing by the congregation of a 'New Christian'- a converted Jew - who scoffed at the idea that they had witnessed a miracle. Two of the friars incited a mob and over three days several hundred Jews were killed. The Inquisition with its cells was established at Rossio's Estaus palace - since demolished - and this area was the scene of several *Autos-da-fé*. The Neo-Manueline **station**, with its horseshoe portals, is off the square to the left of the Theatre. Beyond the station is **Praça dos Restauradores** which has an **obelisk** commemorating the expulsion of the Spanish and the country returning to rule by a Portuguese king. Top left of the elongated square by Avenida da Liberdade, the old funicular the **Ascensor da Glória** takes you to Rua São Pedro de Alcântara and the Bairro Alto district (see below). To the right of Rossio Square is **Praça da Figueira** – another elegant square with some classic refreshment possibilities - again totally rebuilt following the 1755 earthquake – with an equestrian **statue** of King João I. Several bus and tram lines are served.

Santa Justa Elevator

Just off Rua Aurea, south of Rossio Square, you have the chance to take Lisbon's iconic **Santa Justa Elevator**. The 45 metre high iron tower was built by engineer Raoul Mesnier du Ponsard, often claimed to have been a student of Gustav Eiffel, and opened in 1902. It solved the problem of the more tortuous connection between the low-lying streets of the Baixa and the higher part of the Chiado district. The main attraction once you reach the top is the **Convento do Carmo**. At the time one of the most important monasteries in Portugal, its church dedicated to Our Lady of Mount Carmel was devastated by the 1755 earthquake and a resulting fire. This Gothic monument was left in its ruined state, apparently as a reminder of the tragedy that befell the city. There is a small **Archaeologcal Museum** with a collection of finds from several eras.

CHIADO AND BAIRRO ALTO

The top of the Santa Justa elevator also gives easy access to the **Church and Museum of São Roque**. Otherwise it is a case of walking or driving up or down the three streets that form a continuous spine from Praça Duque de Terceira near the river to R. do Alecrim, to R. da Misericórdia and then R. São Pedro de Alcântara. As a general rule, walk up if you want night-time bustle and a meal, down if you want culture. The church is in a square just where the second and last (and highest) of these meet. The Baroque and Mannerist interior of Portugal's first Jesuit church is generally stunning, however it contains one of the masterpieces of European church art. The last of the side chapels on the left before the sacristy entrance and the High and Reliquary altars - **São João Batista** - was commissioned in Rome by King João V in 1740; it was consecrated by the Pope before being sent to Lisbon by ship and reassembled. The wall panels and the floor of the chapel are all mosaic. That is the expensive option by every means! The upright tomb of the English Catholic recusant St Francis Tregian, unusually, is the column of the pulpit. The *trompe l'oeil* ceiling is in the Mannerist style. The chapel of São Roque contains a full size statue of the patron. The museum (€2.50) contains more relics and paintings in addition to those in the church.

Working our way down on the left, the **Church of Our Lady of Loreto** was built by Portuguese but with the influence and help of Italians who had links with the city. The 14th century church was replaced by the present structure in the 17th century. The statuary is both by Italian craftsmen and Italian influenced. We will now take a detour, turning left onto Largo Chiado which runs into Rua Garrett. On the right we have one of the most sacred churches to *Lisboêtas*. The

Basilica dos Mártires features a series of altarpieces honouring those who fell during the reconquest of the city. Afonso Henriques built a chapel on this site honouring a statue of the Virgin brought by his crusader allies who became known as Our Lady of the Martyrs. The first baptism is reputed to have taken place here in the same year as the reconquest. Sage green is the prominent colour of the beautifully light ceiling – another by de Carvalho. Opposite is one of Lisbon's most famous cafes, *A Brasileira*. This area - now recovered from a devastating fire in 1988 - is known for its literary connections and seated at a table outside is a statue of one poet, Fernando Pessoa, while on a pediment is another, António Ribeiro. Along the street and left

São João Batista chapel

onto Calçada Sacramento, the **Church of Sacramento** was restored in 2009 and has painted ceilings, and a crypt containing mummified bodies. Behind the Basilica on R. Serpa Pinto is the **National Theatre of São Carlos**, the opera house opened in 1793.

Back where R. da Misericórdia becomes R do Alecrim, it's another major meeting point. **Camões Square** is on the opposite side of the road, with one side running into Rua Loreto, opposite the Italian church. Following along this road and Calçada do Combro for five minutes – or on Tram 28 – leads us on another detour, but to a stunning church. The interior of the **Church of Santa**

Catarina is a beauty, with stuccoed rococo ceiling and the gilding extending to an elaborate organ surround. Just on the opposite corner of Largo Chiado, meanwhile, is the **church of Nossa Senhora da Encarnação**. The original church was constructed in 1702 and restored in 1784. Like the Loreto church, parts of the medieval walls were demolished and other parts incorporated into the church, in accordance with the Marquês de Pombal reconstruction plans. There are images of St Catherine on the façade, while the statue of Our Lady on the main altarpiece is by Machado de Castro.

Up the streets above São Roque church, cafes mingle with antique shops and boutiques. The **Miradouro de São Pedro de Alcântara** is an atmospheric vantage point at night, and is where you can catch or alight from the Glória funicular. Opposite you have a choice: the **Convent of São Pedro** is worth a look, while at the **Port Wine Institute** you can sample from many examples of the famous fortified wine. Behind the smart main street is a network of narrow streets with bars and keenly priced restaurants. Further to the west, the **Convento dos Cardaes** (Rua de O Século) has a lovely interior. It somehow survived the earthquake, and so too the sisters abduction during the 1910 revolution. The nuns run guided tours and sell produce from their garden. Open Mon.-Fri. 2.30 to 5.30PM; Entrance €5.

Basilica of the Martyrs

OUT FROM MARQUÊS DE POMBAL

Here we list some of the sights in the areas that spread out from the older districts closest to the river. Fronting the northwest side of Marquês de Pombal is the **Parque Eduardo VII** renamed in honour of the British King who visited in 1903. It seems as though all of Lisbon's parks are botanic gardens to a greater or lesser extent, and this park has a 'cold' greenhouse, the *Estufa Fria* in addition to hot houses. At the top end of the park and across right, past the shopping centre brings us to the buildings and gardens of the **Gulbenkian Museum**. Lisbon has a large selection of museums - this comes very highly recommended. Carlouste Gulbenkian was an oil millionaire of Armenian extraction who became a British citizen. He moved to Lisbon in 1942 and determined his stunning private art collection would be displayed. There is sculpture, paintings, ceramics, furniture, carpets and tapestries from early Egyptian through Greek, Islamic, Asian to Art Nouveau. Of the paintings, there are Old Masters, Turners, the Barbizon school and Impressionists. One of the highlights is a room full of Lalique jewellery. Behind the main museum, the **Modern Art Centre** displays Portuguese and foreign paintings. The Gulbenkian Foundation funds education, science and an orchestra. €10-€14 (one or both museums); free on Sunday afternoons.

The **Águas Livres Aqueduct** –starts from Praça das Amoreiras where there is a **museum** but it extends for 58Km and crosses over the expressway Norte-Sul. It was built by order of King João V to bring uncontaminated water to the people of the city. Its 109 arches survived the 1755 earthquake. On R. Rosa Araújo, there is yet another superb private collection at the **Medeiros e Almeida Museum** with Chinese porcelain and many clocks the highlights, among Old Masters, French furniture and exquisite panelling. Entrance: €5; Saturday mornings free; closed Sundays. The large **Botanic Garden** at R. Escola Politécnica - between Av.de Liberdade and southeast of Rato district - is part of the University of Lisbon. Dating from 1858, it has many rare plants from Brazil to Australia.

Southwest of Rato (or Trams 25, 28) lies the **Basilica of Estrela**. It was built by order of Queen Maria I in gratitude for bearing a son and heir, José. Dedicated to the Sacred Heart of Jesus, the church was consecrated in 1789, by which time José had died. The Baroque/Neoclassical exterior features twin towers, a façade decorated with statues of saints, and a large dome. The inside is decorated with coloured marble. The Queen's imperial-style tomb is directly in front of a room housing a remarkable Nativity scene. The **Estrela Gardens** are another of Lisbon's semi-tropical oases, with the English cemetery on the far side. The **Prazeres Cemetery** with its elaborate tombs is west of here, while the Neoclassical palace housing the **National Assembly** is east.

RIBEIRA AND ACROSS THE BRIDGE

In either direction, Lisbon's riverside provides access to yet more highlights. We should start at the **Museu Nacional do Azulejo** – or the Tiles Museum – and the **Madre de Deus Church** (R. Madre de Deus; Bus 794 from Praça do Comércio). The two are in a former convent with the exhibits mostly in the galleries of the large cloister. The Convent of the Mother of God was founded in 1509 by Queen Leonor, widow of King João II. Her tomb is at the entrance to a separate chapel, while the rich decoration of the church was added under later kings. The **chapel of St Anthony**, off the High Choir, has 27 scenes from the Saint's life. The museum displays tiles from the late 15th century to the present day. There are multi-coloured geometric patterns, religious panels – some for altarpieces – and pastoral scenes. The earlier centuries are on the ground floor; however a distinct highlight is the upper gallery which has around its walls a panoramic view of Lisbon c.1700. Entrance: €5; free first Sunday in the month. Back towards the centre, the **Military Museum** is in the former Royal Arsenal next to Santa Apolónia train station and opposite the Cruise Terminal. There is a large collection of artillery, King João I's sword and a room dedicated to Vasco da Gama. Closed Sundays and Mondays.

Going towards the suspension bridge, the **Museum of Ancient Art** (R. Janelas Verdes) is the national museum and gallery. The triptych, Temptations of St Anthony by Hieronymous Bosch, Dürer's St Jerome and Cranach the Elder's Salome with the Head of John the Baptist are but three of the priceless works. The Monstrance of Belém is made of gold brought back by Vasco da Gama. Japanese screens depict the arrival of Portuguese explorers. Entrance: €6

Exhibits at the Tiles Museum

Lisbon's **25th April Suspension Bridge** is very similar to San Francisco's Golden Gate Bridge, though 460m shorter in total. American companies were also involved in Lisbon. Opened in 1966, the bridge connects with the Setúbal peninsular then on to the Algarve. Capacity now comprises six traffic lanes and a rail line; walking and cycling are not possible at time of writing. A toll (€1.75) is charged from south to north only. Before one even crosses, there is another

sense of *Deja vu* that is likely to cause mild confusion. A huge statue of Christ the King - **Cristo Rey** - bears a strong resemblance to the statue of Christ the Redeemer in Rio de Janeiro.The Cardinal Patriarch of Portugal, Cerejeira, was keen on seeing a similar statue erected in Lisbon, when in 1940 he called all the bishops together in Fátima to make a vow that if Portugal was spared from the war, a monument dedicated to the Sacred Heart of Jesus would be erected. Construction took 10 years, with the dedication of the statue taking place on Pentecost 1959 in front of the image of Our Lady of Fátima. It stands on top of a water tower and over a giant cistern, part of the public works programme of the *Estado Novo*. Inside the entrance to climb to the statue are two paintings, one portraying the Consecration of the World to the Immaculate Heart of Mary by Saint John Paul II in 1984, and another portraying the fall of the Berlin Wall. A chapel is dedicated to Our Lady of Peace, there is a chapel of the Blessed Sacrament – both with works including the final apparition and Third Secret of Fátima - and a hall displays paintings recalling the pope, Saint John XXIII's Encyclical *Pax in Terris*. The elevator rises to a landing and staircase to an outside viewing area atop the tower. Before the stairs, a chapel is dedicated to the Confidants of the Heart of Jesus – with relics of Saint Margaret Mary and of Blessed Maria do Divino Coração, to whom Jesus requested that the Pope consecrate all mankind to His Divine Heart. Open every day; arrive by 6PM to climb the monument; entrance fee not covered by the Lisbon Card. Access to the site is in Almada – from the bridge exit, drive round and through the town centre before exiting the roundabout left by the Tram stop, then left again to climb.

Part 14
ESTORIL CASCAIS AND SINTRA

This area is effectively a sub-region of Lisbon and has much to offer the visitor. The 'Estoril Coast' has some of Portugal's best beaches – though if on a day trip for sun and sand consider those between Lisbon and Estoril. The south facing beaches are sandy and the waters generally calm, until they meet the open Atlantic rollers facing west where they are known as a surfers' paradise. There are coastal fortifications all along the wide approaches to Lisbon built to guard against the Spanish, French, English, pirates and privateers, attracted by the empire's riches. Queen Maria II and her husband King Ferdinand established a summer home in the mid 19th century, and from then on, many mansions and villas were built. The resorts became known as a 20th century playground for exiled foreign royalty, the rich and famous, with one of the largest casinos in Europe and world-class venues for golf, yachting, motorsport and tennis. Estoril's neighbour Cascais retains – just about – the atmosphere of a fishing village with more history and a wider choice of accommodation and eating. Up among verdant hills with its own microclimate, lies enchanting Sintra, its fairytale palaces are a must-see for every visitor at some time in their lives. And to cap it all, you can gaze across the Atlantic at Cabo da Roca, the most westerly point of mainland Europe. The coast is served by a cheap, scenic rail line from Cais do Sodré Station in Lisbon, via Belém and Oeiras (30 minutes to Estoril). Journeys to Sintra begin at Rossio Station (40 minutes). €2.20 each way; children half fare.

ESTORIL

There is more than one Estoril, former village centres of São Pedro and São João to the east and Monte Estoril to the west, along the hills above the coast road - Avenida Marginal (N6) - with exploration rewarded by views of fine mansions and the sea. The focal point is the **Casino**, located in gardens leading down to the road, main Estoril rail station, promenade and principal beach, **Praia do Tamariz**. Apart from the obvious slots and tables, there is a theatre, show lounge, art gallery and exhibition space, so it is worth checking out the varied programme. It was rebuilt after World War Two, when it gained a reputation as a hangout for spies from both sides of the conflict who gathered in neutral Portugal. Indeed it served as inspiration for Ian Fleming's first James Bond novel, *Casino Royale* as Fleming had visited the Casino while working in British Naval Intelligence. On the east side of the beach, the **Forte da Cruz** was built in the 17th century during the reign of King Philip III (IV of Spain). It was turned into a villa in the 19th century by the wealthy João Martins de Barros – who commissioned an Italian architect – for the health of his ailing wife. This landmark remains in the same family and is hired out as a corporate and wedding venue.

Back on the opposite side of the Avenida lies Estoril's principal church, **Santo António**. It is part of – and adjacent to – a school complex run by the Salesians of Don Bosco. It was built as a Franciscan monastery on the site of an earlier hermitage. Rebuilt twice since, the earlier remains include the tiles in the porch, with the painted ceiling a 20th century addition. Up in the southern foothills of the Sintra mountains, north of the motor racing circuit (N9 / N9-1) lies the former monastery and church of **Penha Longa**. With Manueline origins, the architecture displays a transition mainly between Mannerist and Baroque. It was a founding monastery of the order of St Jerome and received royal patronage. A national monument, it is nowadays in the shadow of the prestigious golf resort.

CASCAIS

West of and adjoining Estoril, it is not long before arriving in the historic centre of Cascais, whether driving or walking along the promenade. There are plenty of restaurants, cafes and bars in streets and squares leading to the harbour beach, **Praia da Ribeira de Cascais**. The **Palácio Seixas** stands on one side of the beach. It is another fort turned villa now belonging to the Navy. On the

opposite side (southeast) with the fishing boats below, the street climbs up Av. Dom Carlos I towards the **Citadel**. The medieval fortress was captured in 1580 by Spanish forces during the claim of Philip II to the crown of Portugal. He realised that the inadequate defences

Harbour beach, Cascais

Praia da Guincho

needed strengthening, and so a Renaissance battery and barracks on star shaped plan was constructed. The **Palace** of the Citadel served first as a royal residence from 1870 and then of the President of the Republic; you can now take a guided tour (Wed.-Sun.) following restoration. The barracks have been converted into a *Pousada* hotel. Below the fort is the **Marina**. We now make some visits using the Citadel as the focal point.

Across the roundabout at the end of Av. Dom Carlos I on the site of a convent is the brightly coloured **Cultural Centre** which has permanent and temporary exhibits. Walking across gardens to the opposite side of the wide Av. República, there are two more museums. **Casa das Histórias Paula Rego** is worth seeing for the building itself: the structure has two red sandstone coloured chimney-like protrusions resembling those at the National Palace, Sintra. The transition of styles of the acclaimed Portuguese London-based artist might not be to everybody's taste. The small **Museu do Mar** is worth a look for the insights it provides to the maritime traditions of the town. Going back across the roundabout and up Largo Assunção we come to the **parish church** of Cascais. It has paintings by Josefa d'Óbidos. Further along and off left, the **Church of Our Lady of the Navigators** (*dos Navegantes*) has a more ornate Baroque façade, gilded altarpieces and tiled sacristy. It was the fishermen's church.

Returning towards the roundabout we can either proceed down Av. Rei Humberto II – named after the exiled king of Italy who lived here many years – or walk through the Parque Marechal Carmona with its **chapel of San Sebastian** – part of the first of two museum houses. **Museu Condes de Castro Guimarães** is the former home and collection of Irishman George O'Neil, a tobacco magnate who, it is said, lost it while gambling with the Count. The Library contains an illustrated manuscript on the life of Portugal's first king, Afonso Henriques. We come, left, to the **Casa de Santa Maria & Lighthouse**. Another of O'Neil's fantasies, the first phases were designed by Raul Lino in 1902 with strong Moorish/Mozarabic influences. The neighbouring lighthouse contains the original lenses and an exhibition on the life and duties of the keeper. Most museums in Cascais are free and are closed Mondays. www.visitcascais.com

National Palace, Blazons Hall ceiling

Swan room ceiling

wherever the king might be. After Dinis' initial works - including the Palatine chapel with its mosaic floor - the main layout was constructed during the reign of King João I (1385-1433) around the central patio and includes many of the state rooms. The east wing was added in the early 16th century by King Manuel I with his distinctive style decorating the six main windows, and decorating the Palace with a profusion of some of the finest Portuguese tiles. Highlights include the 72 family heraldic shields on the coffered dome of the Blazons Hall, the Swan Room named for the painted ceiling, and similarly, the Magpie Room. Here the story goes that João had the magpies painted after Queen Philippa caught him kissing a lady in waiting. Each bird represents a lady at court after the King's excuse that they were all his virtuous subjects. The **Town Hall** - *Camara Municipal* - is between the Palace and rail station and was built at the turn of the 20th century. Whilst being flamboyant for a public building with its outsize clock tower with matching smaller spires, it fits the spirit of the town.

The journey to the heights of **Pena National Palace** opens up Sintra's natural setting of hills, granite boulders and an abundance of Mediterranean and sub tropical plants. Originally this was the site of a shrine to Our Lady of Pena, with a later (1503) Hieronymite monastery built in the Manueline style. This was partly destroyed in the Lisbon earthquake; however the chapel and

altarpiece by Nicolas Chanterene of the Coimbra school survived, along with the cloisters. The site lay abandoned until the Germanic Ferdinand II, consort to Queen Maria, bought it and commissioned amateur architect and mining engineer Baron Wilhelm Ludwig von Eschwege to design a palace styled as a castle. Construction began in 1842, a fantasia of turrets, battlements, towers, minarets and domes. Nevertheless, with Ferdinand and Maria involved at every stage, there was a deliberate mixing of styles, with some referencing of Portuguese history but with the emphasis on the artistic. Pena Palace might put one in mind of the castles of the Rhine and France that were already there for inspiration, however, the resemblance of Pena to the castles built by the Bavarian 'mad' King Ludwig II later on in the same century is perhaps inescapable.

Once through the entrance gateways and up the 'drawbridge' you are in the main courtyard and are confronted with several distinct buildings linked together. Over the gateway with twin towers is a carved triton, an allegory of the Creation. The neighbouring gateway has candlestick pillars and its façade completely covered in geometric tiles. To the right is a Moorish arched cloister that fronts the older cloister and chapel of the monastery. To the left, from the yellow-coloured cylindrical dome, are the state rooms, which are more traditional than the exterior, but have their curiosities nonetheless.

The surrounding Park has a great

Pena Palace

many attractions, which can be explored as time allows. It can also be a good idea to walk back down to the town through the park. It was planted at the same time as the palace was built, with trees from every corner of the world. To Cruz Alta with its intertwined stone Cross are chapels, a rotunda 'temple' on the site of an earlier chapel and a grotto used by the monks for meditation. A Statue of the Warrior looks down on Ferdinand's creation. Diagonally to the opposite side of the Palace the Valley of the Lakes is reached through forest, or via a separate entrance from the road. Close by are the Hot House, another rotunda and the Queen's Fern Valley. After the Queen died, Ferdinand married the Countess of Edla, and the **Chalet** she had built is on the east side of the Park, again with an alternate entrance from the road (additional admission).

Close to the main entrance to Pena lies the main entrance (ticket office) to the **Moorish Castle**, which Ferdinand restored and embellished as part of his romantic project. There are also pathways from the palace, or alternatively it can be reached by a two Km walk from the town (Rua Marechal Saldanha). Either way, it's a steep climb. The first Sintra church built after the reconquest – São Pedro de Cannaferim – is outside the curtain wall but inside the second circle of walls built to protect the medieval Islamic and Christian communities who settled there, the subject of ongoing archaeological works. Finds and explanations are on display in the church. There are commanding views of the whole sub-region and much more to discover in around the castle, for those with the time and the energy.

Third on the must-see list is **Quinta da Regaleira**. If neither taking the Tourist Bus nor with a group, it is a 15 minute walk up alongside R. Barbosa do Bocage (N 375) from the historic centre, which leads further to Quintinha de Monserrate. The road is narrow with two-way traffic. There is limited parking further along from the Quinta or at the second Tivoli hotel – Seteais Palace. Between 1898 and 1912 Brazilian millionaire António Carvalho Monteiro transformed the site into an exquisitely carved neo-Manueline stone marvel. He commissioned the Italian set designer Luigi Manini as his architect. The estate contains allegories to metaphysics, mythology, Masonry and the Knights Templar (Order of Christ). The house has its beauties, including the dining room fireplace, murals, and portraits of 24 kings and queens. However impressive the house might be, it merely serves as a balcony to the gardens. Not only are there many intriguing man-made structures among the trees above ground, but a network of underground passageways, one of which comes out at the bottom of a 27 metre deep 'initiatic well'. It is great fun to explore even if one is left wondering what it all means. One of the highlights, undoubtedly, is the chapel dedicated to the Holy Trinity. There are stuccoes above the main and side entrances, a beautifully carved altar with a fresco of Christ crowning the Virgin Mary, and further frescoes of St Teresa of Ávila and St Anthony preaching his Sermon to the Fish. The floor mosaic shows the Cross of the Order of Christ over

Gardens of Regaleira Palace

the armillary sphere. As mentioned, nearby **Seteais Palace** serves as a hotel - with palatial trappings and rates. The Neoclassical palace was built in the late 18th century for the Dutch Consul but was sold 10 years later to the Marquis of Marialva. The triumphal arch that connects the two wings was added in 1802 to honour the Prince Regent João VI and Princess Carlota Jaoquina. The well preserved interiors include French frescoes. **Quintinha de Monserrate** (€8) is r e c o m m e n d e d . Influenced by a succession of Englishmen, from William Beckford and Lord Byron, to industrialist Francis Cook (created Viscount of Monserrate by King Luís I) who worked with landscape painter William Stockdale and master gardener Francis Burt, it blends Portugal's Moorish heritage with Indian influences in a sublime setting of parkland and

Chapel of the Holy Trinity

botanic gardens. A similar Moorish revival style is on display back at the **Quinta do Relógio** (Largo da Quinta do Relógio – opp. Regaleira); however at time of writing the palace and gardens are closed.

Elsewhere in Sintra, the **Convento dos Capuchos** is up near Pena Park. While it is unique, with its monks' cells carved into the rock and lined with cork, it is currently subject to long-term restoration and yet still commands the high entrance charge demanded by Parques de Sintra. As such it is under-visited; nevertheless, should you have time to pop in you will see another aspect to this remarkable area and like all monuments under this public-private company's care you are contributing to preserving world heritage. The **Ramalhão Palace** is at the entrance to the town next to the crossing under the **aqueduct**. Nowadays a convent school, it was built by King Dinis and is best known for being where Queen Carlota-Joaquina, the Spanish mother of King Pedro IV was kept under arrest for plotting for Pedro's brother Miguel to usurp the throne. Sintra's churches include **Santa Maria** (off Calçada dos Clérigos) another early church, mainly of Romanesque / Gothic construction. **São Martinho** probably dates from the same period but has more 18th century features. It is in the historic centre.

São Pedro de Penaferrim is a village outside Sintra that is famous for its fair. Its church has 16th and 18th century elements, and there is an ancient hospital.

MAFRA AND ERICEIRA

In this book we have covered the extraordinary wealth brought to the country by the Portuguese discoveries and empire, and the resulting opulence of the many royal palaces, while at the same time covering, briefly, the downfall of the monarchy. Perhaps these things are not entirely unrelated. It was from Mafra and then Ericeira that the royal family departed into exile on October 5th 1910 after the republic was established. One of the last great palaces built is the most gargantuan, the largest Baroque building in Portugal. You can find it – indeed can hardly miss it and it's fun to drive past – by visiting the town of Mafra, 30 minutes' drive north of Sintra. It is then good to go on to the fishing town of Ericeira, whose heritage is active and well preserved and whose dozen or so fishermen's shops have evolved into a fish and seafood lovers' heaven.

Mafra National Palace was ordered by King João V flush with Brazilian gold and constructed from 1717 over a 13-year period by more than 50,000 workers. Johann Freidrich Ludwig was the principal architect and he incorporated German and Italian influences. Following a royal tradition, the Palace was also a monastery, with a church as its centrepiece that became a Basilica. José I established a sculpture school under the Italian Alessandro Giusti to fit out the church. João VI commissioned the six – yes six - organs. The later successors to João V did not much care for the Palace, although it

Mafra National Palace and Basilica of Our Lady & St Anthony

Part 15
A-Z OF PRACTICAL INFORMATION

COMMUNICATIONS

The international dialing code for Portugal is +351. The emergency number is 112. The mobile operators are Meo, Vodafone and Nos. For those travelling around the country that own an unlocked phone, it is well worth investigating limited-time SIM packages from the providers, especially one that allows use of GPS navigation. Shops are in Departures at Lisbon Airport. http://www.vodafone.pt/main/visitingportugal/index/?tab=smartphone Wi-fi internet is widely available in hotels, cafes, shopping centres and petrol stations.

CURRENCY

The currency in Portugal is the Euro (EUR €). Notes are in denominations from 5 to 500 and coins of 1 and 2. There are 100 cents to a Euro with six denominations of coin. **Banks** with exchange facilities in Fátima are mostly situated either side of the Sanctuary in Rua Francisco Marto and Rua Jacinta Marto. Banks and 24-hour ATMs (*MB*) are commonplace throughout the country. Bank opening hours are 8.30AM-3PM Mon-Fri only. VISA, Mastercard and other credit and debit cards are widely accepted.

DRIVING

Portugal drives on the right. The speed limit is 50kph (30mph) in built-up areas, 90kph (54mph) on open roads and 120kph (72mph) on motorways. Use national roads for sightseeing and motorways to get you quickly from point to point.

The motorway network is very good, even though it often appears to take you on a circuitous route. Tolls are payable at regular intervals; unmanned barriers take credit cards and currency but can be temperamental; but some don't – they record the car registration and you are supposed to pay at the post office; you can ask your car hire firm to set you up for the green lane every toll area has so that the tolls are added to your final bill.

The drink driving limit is 50mg of alcohol per 100ml of blood, lower than the UK. Driving manners are some of the poorest in Europe: high speeds, tailgating, flashing and excessive slowness in towns all being commonplace; but actual confrontation is rare.

ELECTRICITY
Standard current is 220V, 50Hz AC. You will need a continental 2-pin adaptor.

EMBASSIES AND CONSULATES
Canada, Australia and Ireland are in the same building (Metro: Avenida) – see below.

The British Consulate is at Rua de São Bernardo 33 1249-082 Lisbon (Nearest Metro: Rato) Tel. 21 392 40 00; e-mail: *ppa.lisbon@fco.gov.uk* for passports or *portugal.consulate@fco.gov.uk* for other matters.

The Irish Embassy is at Avenida da Liberdade 200, 4th floor,1250-147 Lisbon Tel. *21 330 8200.*

The US Embassy is at Avenida das Forças Armadas, Sete-Rios 1600-081; Lisbon Tel. 21 770 2122 e-mail: *conslisbon@state.gov* (Metro: Jardim Zoológico).

The Canadian Embassy is at Avenida da Liberdade 198-200, 3rd Floor 1269-121 Lisbon Tel. 21 316 4600; e-mail: *lsbon@international.gc.ca*

Australia is on the 2nd floor, Avenida de Liberdade 1250-147 Lisbon Tel. 21 310 1500 e-mail: *austemb.lisbon@dfat.gov.au*

New Zealand is represented in Paris, Tel. +33 (0)1 4501 4343 e-mail: *embassy.nz.fr@gmail.com*

South Africa is at Avenida Luís Bívar 10, 1069-024 Lisbon Tel. 21 319 22 00 or 964 151 989 (emergencies only). (Bus 726, 746).

FOOD AND DRINK
We have described local delicacies at various points in the Guide. Good country cooking characterizes Portuguese food – hearty **meat dishes**, stews and soups. The most common meat is pork and offal. **Fish and seafood** are available almost everywhere but come into their own on the coast and by rivers. *Arroz com Gambas* is the famous seafood rice. You will see *Bacalhau* a lot on menus: dried salted cod fish which is then usually added to a sauce and served with vegetables. Avoid *Choco* – it is cuttlefish and is usually very hard. International dishes, particularly Italian, are widely available. Local **cheeses** are well worth seeking out, and it is common to have *queijo da Serra* – a whole round cheese with a creamy centre from the Serra da Estrela Mountains - with bread as a course in a restaurant. Always try the **pastries**, many using egg custard, sometimes almonds, in cafes or pastelaria.

Now to that tetchy subject, how you like your **coffee**. The Italian barista styles are becoming ubiquitous; but where they are not, asking for 'American style' coffee might get you close to what you expect – a large cup of medium strength coffee with milk (hot or cold). Traditionally a *(um) Bica* is a small cup of intense thick coffee requiring plenty of sugar – but now is usually referred to as espresso as it is very similar. *Um Galão* is like a latte served in a glass with a metal cage and handle. *Uma meia de leite* is another milky coffee in a 6oz cup.

Um Pingo is like the Spanish cortado, half espresso and half milk. *Uma Pingado* is practically identical to macchiato. *Um Garoto* is weak, not quite decaff (which is widely available).

Some of the best Portuguese **table wines** come from the Alentejo, the region that has made great strides in recent years. Closer to Fátima, the Ribatejo – or now known as Tejo - produces some excellent wines, red and white, with Almerim, Santarém and Tomar being three of its sub-regions. Look out for Alcobaça and Óbidos wines as well – lightish reds, young whites and sparkling. Northern Portugal is famous for its Port, of course, but some of the Douro is reserved for superior table wines. Further south, the best known red wine is full-bodied Dão. Another famous style from the north is Vinho Verde or 'green wine' meaning young:- refreshing, light in alcohol and with a distinct pétillance – white is the most popular. **Beer** (*'Uma cerveja por favor'*) is mainly of the lager variety: Sagres is a good thirst quencher, while Super Bock has a more intense hoppy flavour, some stronger versions and a stout. For a country that grows citrus fruit naturally, **juices** are perhaps surprisingly not to the fore.

Restaurants add service to the bill; however it is common to leave another 5-10% if you are satisfied. They tend to open from 12-3PM for lunch and 7-10PM for dinner.

MEDICAL ASSISTANCE

Healthcare in Portugal is of a good standard with modern facilities. Dial 112 or ask your hotel reception for help. When out and about, any pharmacy will direct you to a doctor or provide advice for common complaints. EU/EEA citizens should obtain a European Health Insurance Card. This entitles you to basic hospital and doctor treatment; however full travel insurance will be required for ongoing help and repatriation.

PASSPORTS AND VISAS

Portugal is a member of the EU and wider EEA, and the Schengen zone, and so all citizens of these countries enter visa-free. The same applies to citizens of Australia, Brazil, Canada, New Zealand, Singapore, the USA and some other countries. Visas are required from many more, including India and South Africa. You should check on the latest position. Portugal and Spain do not normally operate border posts, customs or passport control on their land borders. The same applies to France but not for those visiting Andorra or coming from the United Kingdom.

PUBLIC HOLIDAYS

In Portugal holidays are numerous; they include certain Feast days and historic anniversaries and result in many services being unavailable. Good Friday and Easter Sunday only; Liberation Day April 25th; Labour Day May 1st; National Day

June 10th; Corpus Christi; Assumption of the Virgin Mary August 15th; Republic Day October 5th; All Saints' Day November 1st; Restoration of Independence December 1st; Feast of the Immaculate Conception December 8th; Christmas Day and New Year's Day. In addition Shrove Tuesday – known as Carnival in Portugal – is an optional holiday.

TIMEZONE
Portugal is in the Western European Time Zone, which means the time is the same as the UK and Ireland, and for most of the year it is five hours ahead of Eastern Time. Spain and France are one hour ahead.

TOURIST INFORMATION
There are offices of Turismo de Lisboa in the Arrivals Hall at Lisbon Airport and throughout the city; in Sintra the office is by the rail station. www.visitlisboa.com Fátima and all of the surrounding attractions are in the Centro Tourism region www.centerofportugal.com The Portuguese National Tourist office www.visitportugal.com has locations in London, Dublin, New York and Toronto.

TRAVEL
For travel on arrival see Lisbon section under VISITING pp. 99-100.

The airlines that serve Lisbon include TAP www.flytap.com who fly from London, Manchester, New York, Boston and Toronto among other cities. Trans-Atlantic services are also operated by American, United, Delta, Air-Transat and Azores Airlines. Besides British Airways and Aer Lingus, carriers from the UK and Ireland include Easyjet and Ryanair. The easiest and cheapest way to get between Madrid and Lisbon without a car (and perhaps better than keeping one hire car the whole trip) is with Easyjet – they haven't yet managed to build a high-speed rail line between the two cities. The other airports on mainland Portugal are Porto and Faro.

WATER
Tap water is safe to drink throughout Portugal. Bottled mineral water (*Água mineral*) comes in still (*sem gás*) or sparkling (*com gás*). See Sanctuary for Fátima water.

WEBSITES
In addition to all of the other websites mentioned in this book, the following should prove useful when planning a trip. For Lisbon: www.lisbonlux.com; www.golisbon.com; www.lisbon.net; www.lisbon-portugal-guide.com has versions for other places, including Sintra and Óbidos. To discover more of the country's cuisine www.foodfromportugal.com and www.winesofportugal.info

Part 16
DEVOTIONS

DAILY PILGRIMS' PROGRAMME

There are at least seven masses and four rosaries per day. The masses are in Portuguese, English, Spanish and Italian. We reproduce the Mass, in part to help English-speaking pilgrims follow it when it is being celebrated in another language; the Rosary is here for collective and individual meditation. Each pastoral year has its own theme, published at the end of November. It is not possible to go into detail in a book such as this, as the theme changes and they are not known very far in advance. A Pilgrim's Itinerary leaflet is produced in several languages, with dispensers around the *Recinto*. The leaflet might give a route, with stations at selected Sanctuary landmarks, with a meditation to accompany each station.

THE ROSARY

Perhaps taken for granted ordinarily, at Fátima we come to devote ourselves to the Lady of the Rosary, the intention being to lift this everyday cycle of prayer and rediscover its significance. The three seers of Fátima were instructed to recite the Rosary every day and were also taught simple prayers by the Angel who appeared to them. During the third apparition (July 13th 1917), Our Lady taught the children a prayer to recite after each Mystery (or decade) of the Rosary.*

At the beginning
(making the sign of the cross)
God come to our aid. Lord, come to our rescue and save us. Glory be to the Father, to the son and to the Holy Spirit. As it is was in the beginning, is now, and ever shall be, world without end.   *Amen*

The Joyful Mysteries
1. The Annunciation (The angel comes to Mary)   Luke 1:26-38
2. The Visitation (Mary visits Elizabeth)   Luke 1:39-56
3. The Birth of Jesus   Luke 2:1-20
4. The Presentation in the Temple   Luke 2:22-38
5. The Finding of the Child Jesus in the Temple   Luke 2:41-50

The Sorrowful Mysteries
1. Prayer and agony in the Garden   Mat. 26:36-46
2. Scourging at the Pillar   Mat. 27:24-26
3. Crowning with Thorns   Mat. 27:27-31
4. On the way to Calvary   Luke 23:26-32
5. Crucifixion and Death   John 19:17-30

The Glorious Mysteries
1. Resurrection   Mat. 28:1-10
2. Ascension   Acts 1:6-11
3. Coming of the Holy Spirit on the Apostles   Acts 1:12-14 & 2:1-4
4. Assumption of Our Lady into heaven   Luke 1:48-49
5. Crowning of Our Lady and Glory of the Saints   Rev. 12:1-17

The Luminous Mysteries
1. Baptism in the Jordan   Mat. 3:13-17
2. Revelation during the wedding at Cana   John 2:1-11
3. Proclamation of God's Kingdom   Mark 1:14-15
4. The Transfiguration   Luke 9:28-36
5. The institution of the Eucharist   Luke 22:14-20

For each Mystery (x5) or decade recite:
one Our Father
ten Hail Marys
one Glory be to the Father
O Mary *(may be said)*
O my Jesus*
concluding with the prayer Hail Holy Queen and the Rosary Prayer or three Hail Marys + Hail Holy Queen.

ROSARY PRAYERS

THE LORD'S PRAYER

Our Father, who art in heaven, hallowed be Thy Name; Thy kingdom come; Thy will be done on earth as it is in heaven. Give us this day our daily bread; and forgive us our trespasses as we forgive those who trespass against us; and lead us not into temptation, but deliver us from evil.   *Amen*

THE HAIL MARY

Hail Mary, full of grace! The Lord is with thee; blessed art thou amongst women, and blessed is the Fruit of thy womb, Jesus. Holy Mary, Mother of God, pray for us sinners, now and at the hour of our death.   *Amen*

THE GLORIA

Glory be to the Father, and to the Son, and to the Holy Ghost; As it was in te beginning, is now, and ever shall be, world without end.   *Amen*

MIRACULOUS MEDAL PRAYER (may be said)

O Mary conceived without sin. Pray for us who have recourse to you.

Amen

DECADE PRAYER*

O my Jesus, forgive us, save us from the fire of hell. Lead all souls to heaven, especially those who are most in need.

HAIL HOLY QUEEN

Hail, holy Queen, mother of mercy; hail, our life, our sweetness, and our hope.To thee do we cry, poor banished children of Eve; to thee do we send up our sighs, mourning and weeping in this vale of tears.Turn then, most gracious advocate, thine eyes of mercy towards us; and after this our exile, show unto us the blessed fruit of thy womb, Jesus.

O clement, O loving, O sweet Virgin Mary.   *Amen*

ROSARY PRAYER

P: Pray for us, O holy Mother of God.

C: That we may be made worthy of the promises of Christ.

Let us pray.

O God, whose only-begotten Son, by His life, death and resurrection, has purchased for us the rewards of eternal life; grant, we beseech thee, that meditating on these mysteries, in the most holy Rosary of the Blessed Virgin Mary, we may both imitate what they contain, and obtain what they promise, through the same Christ our Lord.   *Amen*

FATIMA PRAYERS

PARDON PRAYER
My God, I believe, I adore, I hope and I love You! I ask pardon of You for those who do not believe, do not adore, do not hope and do not love You!

Amen

PRAYER OF THE ANGEL
Most Holy Trinity, Father, Son and Holy Spirit, I adore You profoundly, and I offer You the most precious Body, Blood, Soul and Divinity of Jesus Christ, present in all the tabernacles of the world, in reparation for the outrages, sacrileges and indifference with which He Himself is offended. And, through the infinite merits of His most Sacred Heart, and the Immaculate Heart of Mary, I beg of You the conversion of poor sinners. *Amen*

EUCHARISTIC PRAYER
O most Holy Trinity, I adore You! My God, my God, I love You in the most Blessed Sacrament. *Amen*

SACRIFICE PRAYER
Our Lady taught the children to say a prayer whenever they offered a sacrifice up to God.

O Jesus, it is for love of You, for the conversion of sinners, and in reparation for the sins committed against the Immaculate Heart of Mary. *Amen*

CONSECRATION TO THE IMMACULATE HEART OF MARY
Virgin Mary, Mother of God and our Mother, to your Immaculate Heart we consecrate ourselves, in an act of total entrustment to the Lord.

By You we will be led to Christ. By Him and with Him we will be led to the Father.

We will walk in the light of faith, and we will do everything so that the world may believe that Jesus Christ is the One sent by the Father.

With Him we wish to carry His Love and Salvation to the ends of the earth.

Under the protection of your Immaculate Heart, we will be one People with Christ. We will be witnesses of His Resurrection. By Him we will be led to the Father, for the glory of the Most Holy Trinity, Whom we adore, praise and bless forever. *Amen*

PRAYER FOR THE POPE
O Lord,
Good shepherd of Humanity, who entrusted to Peter and his successors the mission of strengthening the brothers in the faith and to enlighten them in the hearing of the Word

– in this place where the little shepherds of Fatima bore witness to a profound devotion to the Holy Father and to an intense love for the Church –, We ask You that Your Spirit of Wisdom illumines Pope *N* in his mission as the Successor of Peter;

May Your mercy protect and comfort him;

May the testimony of Your faithful hearten him in his mission,

And may the tender presence of Mary be for him a sign of Your love;

May he be strong in faith, courageous in hope, and zealous in charity.

Who live and reign with God the Father, in the unity of the Holy Spirit, one God, for ever and ever.   *Amen*

Our Father. Hail Mary. Glory be to the Father.

FIRST FIVE SATURDAYS PROGRAMME

Every first Saturday of the month the following programme is followed in the Sanctuary for the celebration of the first Saturdays:

11.00AM	Mass, in the Basilica of the Most Holy Trinity
2.00PM	Hour of Reparation to the Immaculate Heart of Mary, in the Chapel of the Apparitions, followed by 15 minutes of company to Our Lady
3.00PM	Meditation and Eucharistic adoration, in the Basilica of the Most Holy Trinity (until 4.00PM)
9.30PM	Recitation of the Rosary, in the Chapel of the Apparitions, and candlelight procession.

THE MASS

The Eucharistic prayers and Communion Rite may be found in a Sunday or Weekday Missal.The penitential rite and readings, homily and bidding prayers (Prayer of the Faithful) are mostly composed or chosen for each individual celebration.

The Mass is composed of five sections.

1. The Introductory Rites   - entrance Chant

- greeting (eg. The grace of our Lord Jesus Christ etc.)
- Pentiential Act (Have mercy on us, O Lord; or Kyrie eleison)
- sometimes followed by a hymn (Glory to God in the highest etc.)
- Silent prayer, followed by the Collect prayer

2. The Liturgy of the Word	- readings, responsorial psalm
	- Alleluia (or other chant depending on liturgical calendar), incense (where used), Cleanse my heart and my lips etc.
	- reading
	- homily
	- creed and bidding prayers
3. The Liturgy of the Eucharist	- preparation of the altar
	- bringing of the gifts (bread and wine)
	- offertory chant; Wash me O Lord etc.
	- 'Pray, brethren (brothers and sisters), that my sacrifice and yours may be acceptable to God, the almighty Father.' R/ 'May the Lord accept the sacrifice at your hands for the praise and glory of his name, for our good and the good of all his holy Church.' Prayer over the offerings.
	- Eucharistic prayer (one of four, some parts can be sung)
4. The Communion Rite	- Our Father
	- sign of peace
	- 'Lamb of God, you take away the sins of the world, have mercy on us (2); grant us peace (1).'
	- 'May the receiving of your Body and Blood, Lord Jesus Christ, not bring me to judgement' etc.
	- Lord, I am not worthy
	- distribution of communion
	- psalm or hymn may be sung
	- silent prayer; Prayer after Communion
5. The Concluding Rites	- announcements
	- dismissal

FATIMA HYMNS

The Basilica's tower chimes the opening bars of Fátima's signature song. António Botto's *Avé de Fátima* is sung during the candlelight procession and masses. The hymn has simplicity and beauty. There have been several attempts to put words to the song in other languages, including more than one English version. Here is one that seems to fit well with the tune.

IN FATIMA'S COVE

1. In Fatima's cove on the thirteenth of May; the Virgin Maria appeared at mid-day.

2. The Virgin Maria surrounded by light; God's Mother is ours for she gives us this sight.

3. The world was then suffering from war, plague, and strife, and Portugal mourned for her great loss of life.

4. To three shepherd children the Virgin then spoke a message so hopeful, with peace for all folk.

5. With sweet Mother's pleading, she asked us to pray, do penance, be modest, the Rosary each day.

6. All Portugal heard what God's Mother did say, converted it sings of that Queen to this day.

7. We all must remember Our Lady's request, do all that she asks for, obey her bequests.

8. She warned of behavior from which we must turn, of thoughts, words, and actions which Christians must spurn.

9. To her sad, sweet pleading our promise is made, that God's Law in all things be strongly obeyed.

10. From nation to nation her fair name is praised, as souls from sin's bondage are contritely raised.

11. Our thanks to the Godhead, whose ways are so sure for giving us Mary, our Mother Most Pure.

12. Our hearts, overflowing with kindness and love, thank her for God's graces bestowed from above.

13. Hail, Refuge of sinners! Hail, Star of the Sea! Hail, Queen of Creation! Our hope is in thee.

14. All hail, Virgin Mary! This Star guides our way, our country's Protectress, America's Way!

Our Lady of Fatima sent from above
appeared to three children to tell of God's love:
Refrain: Ave, Ave, Ave Maria! Ave, Ave, Ave Maria!

While taking part in the farewell procession on October 13th and other anniversaries and singing the hymn *Adeus de Fátima* (Pedro M. R. Caetano) it is traditional for pilgrims and cocelebrants to wave white handkerchiefs.

O FATIMA, FAREWELL!

O Virgin of the Rosary
of Fatima dear Lady,
O dearest Queen of Heaven
to save thou' art ever ready.
O Virgin of the Rosary of Fatima dear
Lady,
As now we leave your sanctuary
once more we kneel before thee.

Before we leave O Mother
oh, hear our prayer of sorrow,
And save us from all danger
today, tonight, tomorrow.
Before we leave, O Mother
have mercy on our sorrow,
And ever be our guardian,
today, tonight, tomorrow.

O Mother as we leave you
the tears to our eyes are springing,
But still our hearts with happiness,
your love, your praise are singing.
O Mother as we leave you
our eyes with tears are dimming,
But though we weep at parting
our souls with love are brimming.

Refrain:
Just one more final prayer
as we leave, O Mother Mary!
May our hearts ever ring
with the words that we sing:
Oh Fatima! Farewell!
Mother dear, Farewell!

At the well of Arneiro: "Make of everything you can a sacrifice, and offer it to God as an act of reparation for the sins by which He is offended, and in supplication for the conversion of sinners. You will thus draw down peace upon your country."

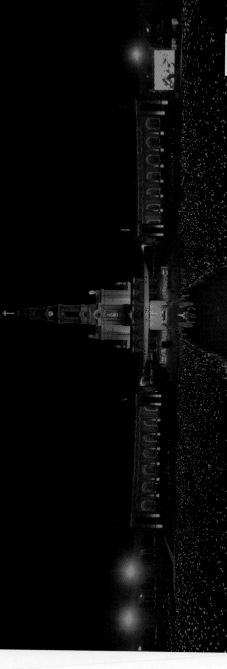

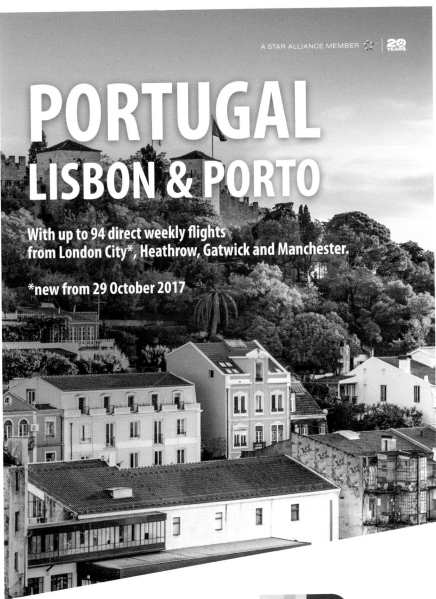

A STAR ALLIANCE MEMBER ✦ | 20 YEARS

PORTUGAL
LISBON & PORTO

With up to 94 direct weekly flights
from London City*, Heathrow, Gatwick and Manchester.

*new from 29 October 2017

flytap.com

Contact Centre: 0345 601 0932
For further information please contact your local travel agent.

TAP PORTUGAL